D0586715

THE FARMERS OF OLD ENGLAND

THE FARMERS
OF OLD ENGLAND

by
Eric Kerridge

London
GEORGE ALLEN & UNWIN LTD
Ruskin House   Museum Street

First published in 1973

© George Allen & Unwin Ltd 1973

ISBN 0 04 942108 5 Hardback
0 04 942109 3 Paperback

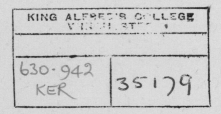
Printed in Great Britain
in 12 point Fournier type
by Unwin Brothers Limited
Woking and London

To Bumble

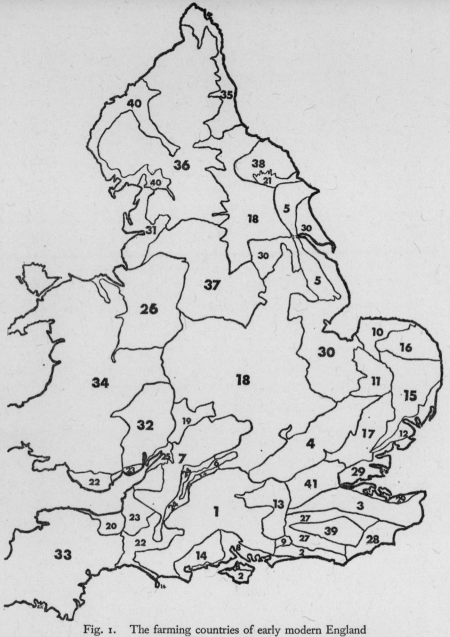

Fig. 1.   The farming countries of early modern England

1 Chalk Country	11 Breckland	22 Butter Country	33 West Country
2 Southdown Country	12 Sandlings Country	23 Western Waterlands	34 Wales
3 Northdown Country	13 Blackheath Country	24 Cheese Country	35 North-eastern
4 Chiltern Country	14 Poor Soils Country	25 Vale of Berkeley	Lowlands
5 Northwold Country	15 High Suffolk	26 Cheshire Cheese	36 North Country
6 Oxford Heights	16 East Norfolk	Country	37 Peak-Forest Country
Country	17 Woodland	27 Wealden Vales	38 Blackmoors
7 Cotswold Country	18 Midland Plain	28 Romney Marsh	39 High Weald
8 South Seacoast	19 Vale of Evesham	29 Saltings Country	40 North-western
Country	20 Vale of Taunton	30 Fen Country	Lowlands
9 Petworth District	Deane	31 Lancashire Plain	41 Vale of London
10 Norfolk Heathlands	21 Vale of Pickering	32 Vales of Hereford	

Acknowledgements

I wish to thank the undermentioned for their kind permission to reproduce illustrations: the Director of the Science Museum, London (*plate 23*), the Keeper of the Public Records (*plate 13*), the General Editor of the *Victoria History of the Counties of England* (*plates 2, 11*), the Clarendon Press (*figures 10, 11* after Orwin and Orwin, *The Open Fields*), Messrs Aerofilms Ltd, London (*plates 1, 17, 18, 19, 20, 21, 22*), Sir Gyles Isham, Bart. (*plate 32*), the Earl of Pembroke (*figure 16*), and the Director of the British Museum. *Figure 10*, and *plates 3, 4, 5, 6, 7, 8, 9, 10, 12, 14, 15, 16, 24, 25, 26, 27, 28, 29, 30, 31* appear by courtesy of the Trustees of the British Museum. All translations, transcriptions and photographs of Crown copyright records in the Public Record Office appear by kind permission of the Controller of Her Majesty's Stationery Office. Thanks are also due to Mrs Lilian Lund, Mrs Meriel Jones, Mr Leonard Jones, Mr Charles Furth, and above all to my wife.

E.K.

Contents

Illustrations

FIGURES

INTRODUCTION

In this book I try to tell the story of the farmers of England, their labourers and their landlords, in the period between about 1560 and 1760, to show how they went about their business, and to recount their great achievements. It was at this time that English farming underwent those mighty and profound changes that set up a unique form of rural life and economy, the peculiar 'rural reign' rejoiced at in the last verse but one of 'Rule Britannia', which was composed towards the end of this period. British agriculture became the wonder and envy of the world. Frenchman and Swede alike were amazed by the sight of rural England. The 'rural reign' helped to make Britain's commerce shine and was a great pillar of strength to the whole nation. It was one of the main causes of England's former wealth and power, and its influence, its example, and its very terminology were spread to the Continent, to the new countries beyond the seas, and to all the western world.

These feats were performed partly by landowners, but above all by the farmers of England, or, rather, by the minority of them who showed initiative and enterprise. That they were able to accomplish so much was due partly to the ground having been so well prepared for them. It was thanks largely to their forbears that free-born Englishmen enjoyed the right to the fruit of their labours. It was thanks to their ancestors that they inherited agricultural techniques already far in advance of those in almost all the rest of the world.

These farmers inherited much, but they created and fashioned far more for themselves, and for others, for the riches they heaped up were shared by their employees and landlords and by the great mass of common people. This is also the story, then, of how the English became an opulent people, of the roast beef of old England, of John Bull's success in the world.

Plate 1 Ridge and Furrow. The distinct pattern of twice or thrice elevated ridge and furrow is as clear today as when these enclosed fields were last laid down to grass. Note how the direction of ploughing tends to follow the slope of the field. (Aerofilms Ltd)

Plate 2 Terraces and linchets. Survivals at Upton St Leonards (Cotswold Country). The terraces appear to have gone out of cultivation and the linchets, no longer being either mown or tethered

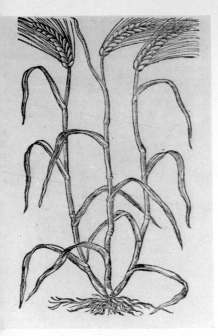

Plate 3 Bigg or beer. The northern winter barley drawn in 1597. (British Museum)

Plate 4 Naked oats (1597). The northern oats grown for bread, porridge and malt. It needed no milling. (British Museum)

Plate 5 The tare or vetch. One of its many varieties shown in a drawing of 1597. It served much the same purpose as clover. Both pods and flowers are shown. (British Museum)

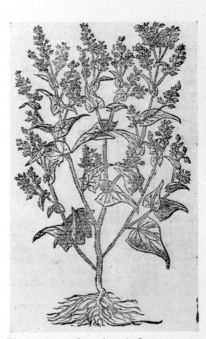

Plate 6 Buckwheat (1597). It was sown for sheep and poultry feed and was ploughed in as green manure. (British Museum)

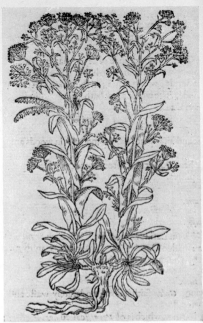

Plate 7 Rape or cole-seed (1597). Grown in drained fens or marshes for sheep-feed and for the oil crushed from the seeds. (British Museum)

Plate 8 Woad (1597). Grown especially as a pioneer crop in newly ploughed up grassland. The leaves were eaten by sheep, but the chief product was dye-stuff. (British Museum)

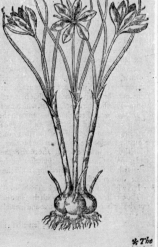

Plate 9 Saffron depicted in and out of flower (1597). Only the stamens were picked and used for condiment and flavouring. (British Museum)

Plate 10 English tobacco (yellow henbane). This drawing, published in 1597, shows the plant that was grown in the Vale of Evesham for pipe-tobacco (British Museum)

Plate 11 Boundary balk with merestone. Part of a boundary balk preserved from
a former common field at Upton St Leonards, complete with merestone engraved
with owner's initial. (By courtesy of *Victoria History*)

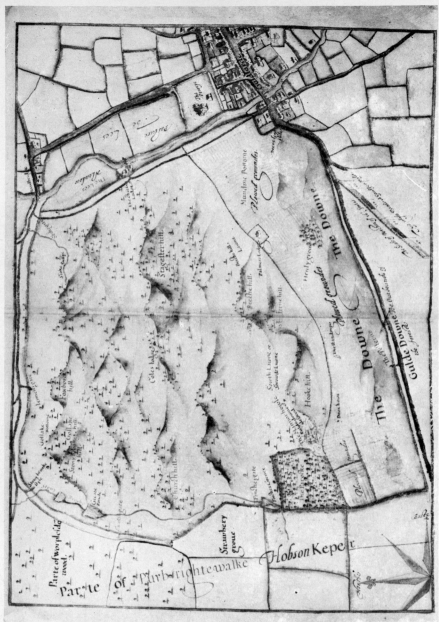

Plate 12 Guildford Park 1607. This map by John Norden shows the park and its palings, about six and a quarter miles in circumference. It lay next to Windsor Forest. The features include the River Wey and the meadows and pastures on its banks, a large part of Guildford town, portions of Worplesdon Wood and of Pirbright Walk in the forest, and the hamlet of Woodbridge. All the lodges and the dwelling houses in both Guildford and Woodbridge have chimney stacks. The manor house has been pulled down, but the dove house still stands. The southern part of the park (slightly north of the Hog's Back), has been fenced off, ploughed up and cast into furlongs, where the various directions of ploughing may be discerned by the hatching used to represent ridges and furrows. (British Museum)

Plate 13 Sheep and cattle about 1606. From a map of Lye Plain in Aldbourne (Chalk Country). The cartographer is intending to represent shire horses, middle-horn cattle and Chalk Country sheep. Observe (bottom) the merestones of a common field and (top left) the new lodge with chimney stacks, tiled roof and dormer rooms. Trees are represented by sprigs of leaves. (By courtesy of the Public Record Office: Maps and Plans, MR.13)

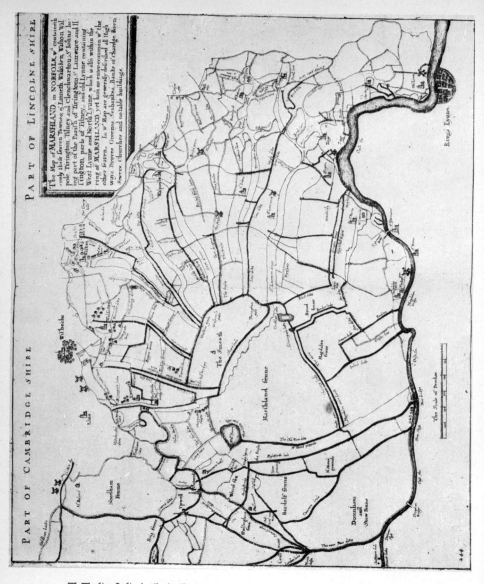

Plate 14 The Marshland district. A map published in 1662. In addition to the drainage sewers and dikes, and the windmills, observe the droveways for live-stock moving to and from the remnants of incom-pletely drained fen. North is to the right of the map. (British Museum)

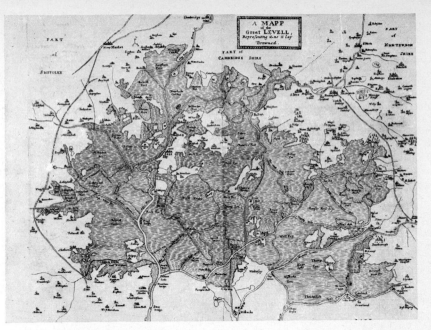

Plate 15 The Great Level 'as it lay drowned' before 1630. As can be seen, however, it was already drained, though incompletely, by numerous delfs and lodes.
East is to the left and north to the bottom. (British Museum)

Plate 16 The Great Level drained to winterground. The new straight cuts to the
sea are unmistakable. Notice the wide washes; these were to accommodate water
that the canals could not take away. (British Museum)

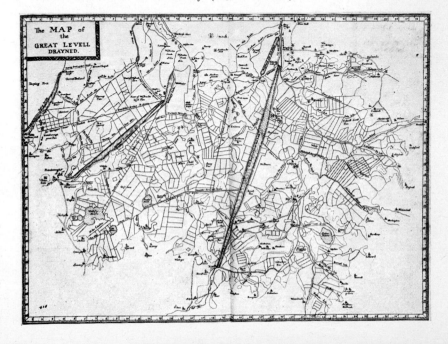

Plate 17 As different as Chalk and Cheese. At the centre, Roundway Down, a promontory of the Chalk Country, with champion fields and sheep-downs. At the top, the Cheese Country, with its woodland landscape of enclosed fields, and its smaller farms. Note a patch of the escarpment that has reverted to scrub in the absence of sheep, the contour ploughing on the lower slopes, and the terraces and linchets on the distant escarpment. (Aerofilms Ltd)

Plate 18 Floated meadows in the Chalk Country (I). Watermeadows floated by the ridge-and-furrow method between Salisbury and West Harnham. The whole lay-out of carriers and drains is clearly visible. When this picture was taken, the hatches were closed and no water was flowing. Note as a reference point, for comparison with plate 19, the Old Mill House at W. Harnham, at 'twelve o'clock'. (Aerofilms Ltd)

Plate 19 Floated meadows in the Chalk Country (II). By reference to the Old Mill House (now at 'nine o'clock') it will be seen that these are largely the same meadows as in plate 18. But now the hatches are open and water is flowing along the stems and carriers, which are still fairly well preserved. Salisbury Cathedral in the foreground. (Aerofilms Ltd)

Plate 20 Floated meadows in the Chalk Country (III). Cut by the railroad, these floated watermeadows at Wilton survive as a monument to former glories. (Aerofilms Ltd). Plate 21 Floated meadows in the Chalk Country (IV). A well preserved pitch of work at Durrington on the Salisbury Avon. (Aerofilms Ltd). Plate 22 Floated meadows in the Chalk Country (V). Some more of the ridge-and-furrow meadows laid out by the old floaters at Wilton near Salisbury. (Aerofilms Ltd)

Plate 23 Ploughing with oxen in the Middle Ages. Two yokes of oxen, a plain-country plough, a ploughman and driver, workers breaking clods, and corn harvesters in the background. From the diorama in the Science Museum, based on illustrations in the Luttrell Psalter (fourteenth century) in the British Museum. (By courtesy of Science Museum, London)

Plate 24 Ploughing with horses in the seventeenth century (I). A pair of horses, a plain-country plough, and a solitary ploughman. The horses are wearing plumes. The ploughman's long hair is typical of the period (1652). Clothing is shown in the authentic fashion. An English ploughshare intrudes at the top of the drawing. (British Museum)

Plate 25 Ploughing with horses in the seventeenth century (II). A drawing made about twenty years later than the previous one and equally true to life. (British Museum). Plate 26 Harrowing (1669). A crude but authentic drawing. (British Museum). Plate 27 Broadcasting the seed (1669). A successful angler in the background. (British Museum). Plate 28 Setting hurdles for the sheep-fold. Driving in the rods to hold the wattle-hurdles. The broad-brimmed hat, smock, baggy breeches, stockings, shoes, and long hair are typical of the mid-seventeenth century. (British Museum). Plate 29 Cutting the corn with a sickle (1660s). The men are wearing jerkins or waistcoats. (British Museum). Plate 30 Mowing the hay with a scythe (1660s), in shirt-sleeves. (British Museum).

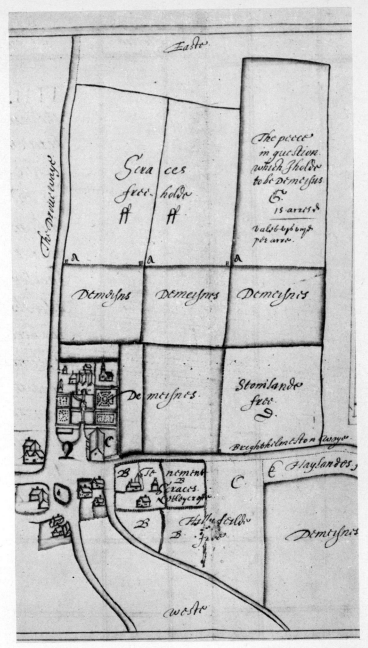

Plate 31 The village of Preston 1607, shown in John Norden's plan. Situated in the Southdown Country just north of Brighton (Brighthelmeston) and on Brighthelmeston Way. The village houses have dormer rooms, chimneys and red tiled roofs. In the village square is what seems to be one of the new-fangled water pumps set up for the use of the inhabitants. (British Museum)

Plate 32 The village of Haselbeech 1600. A village in the Midland Plain depicted in a map made to show the new allotments when the township was enclosed. These houses, too, have chimneys, dormer rooms and red tiled roofs. (By courtesy of Sir Gyles Isham, Bart.)

Chapter One

THE COUNTRYSIDE

The first task that faced country-people in Britain was no less than the taming of a wilderness. In its original state the land was of no use for agriculture. In some places poor and in others rich, the soil produced vegetation that was either sparse and stunted or lush and rank, but nowhere was it ready and prepared for the farmer. The poorer the land, the greater the pains needed to make it fertile for crops; the richer the land, the more difficult it was to clear for cultivation. Here lay impenetrable thickets, there impassable marshes, and all parts were equally the domain of wild and often dangerous beasts and reptiles. Like America, Australia and other 'new' countries, it at first suited only the hunter and the collector. We shall never know how many generations of men spent their lives in pursuit of game and fish and in gathering wild fruits and plants. We can only be sure that they did not live entirely in vain, and that they at least helped to curb the worst excesses of nature just enough to smooth the path for the herdsman and the tiller of the soil. When we first take up the story, in the earliest historical times, England was already many stages removed from a state of nature and its people were far advanced in that taming of the wilderness that preoccupied them in the early Middle Ages. It was only over many centuries that successive generations of husbandmen painfully and laboriously made the soils, fields and countryside to their own needs and liking. Man did not create the world, but he made his own environment. The countryside we are accustomed to regard as natural is as man-made as a motorway or an oil refinery.

Champion and Woodland

This countryside, when fashioned, was possessed of an almost infinite variety, the full description of which would defy a million pens; but certain broad features were shared by countless otherwise unique sites and spots and allowed them to be roughly classified as either 'champion' or 'woodland'. The former consisted of vast, unbroken plains, and the latter of great chequerboards of enclosed fields. These were what had been made out of lands that in their wild state had been respectively either too poor and bare or too rich and rank to serve the husbandman's turn. The champion was largely clean and dry, the woodland dirty and miry. As the old saying went, the one was good for the rider, and the other for the abider (*plate 17*).

The spacious sheep-pastures that covered much or most of the chalk downs radiating from Salisbury Plain as far as the Dorset, South and North Downs, the Cromer Ridge and the Yorkshire Wolds, as well as wide areas on the Cotswolds and the Oxford Heights, were all made and maintained in that state by the dwellers in the downland and other valleys, merely by feeding their sheep upon them day after day. The downs, 'in their flowing forms resembling vast, pale green waves, wave upon wave "in fluctuation fixed" ' (W. H. Hudson), did not naturally present John Milton with the spectacle of 'level downs, and flocks grazing the tender herb'. As Hudson explains,

'The sheep fed closely, and everything that grew on the down, grasses, clovers, and numerous small creeping herbs, had acquired the habit of growing and flowering close to the ground, every species, and each individual plant, striving, with the unconscious intelligence that is in all growing things, to hide its leaves and pushing sprays under the others, to escape the nibbling teeth by keeping closer to the surface.'

Now that the sheep have been ousted, we can see something of what the downs would have been like before the arrival of the shepherds with their flocks. Once the sheep have gone for good, the herbs and grasses know no fear, least of all of the cows, which only wrap their tongues around the top of the sward. Then the plants boldly stretch up to the light and form a mat of coarse, clumpy vegetation studded with bushes and stunted trees (*plate 17*). Once this has happened, the downs are no place for tender-mouthed ewes and lambs. They would sooner starve than eat such fare. Thus, step by step, is destroyed that close-cropped, thick-piled carpet of verdure that the old sheep flocks had slowly unrolled and laid beneath their own feet.

It was similar with the heathlands. At first they were the wild, unkempt wastes that we know today, only more widespread, none of them yet having been planted in geometrical patterns of outlandish pines and firs. Then came the shepherds with their flocks, and hundreds and thousands of nibbling jaws killed in the quick the shoots of furze, gorse, broom, bracken and brambles, and cropped and encouraged the mat of sweet heather. The heaths were then aptly named; they grew some thin grass, but mostly heath.

Elsewhere the deep, moist plains and vales gave rise to thick woods of oak and other trees, interspersed with grassy glades. Most of this wood-pasture land was too wet for sheep during a great part of the year, but gave rich, lush grazing for cows. Here most of the farmland was enclosed directly from the original woods, whose ragged remnants served as hedge and coppice-rows to bound the small closes that went to make up this 'arden' or woodland countryside. Yet it was not by axe and fire alone that the woods were cleared, for the farmer's animals, including his sheep in summer, sauntered about, eating off the new shoots as they came and preventing the growth of trees. Even so, many of the woods were preserved in more or less their original state, because most of the royal forests, which were hunting-grounds and game-reserves, included large areas of wood-pasture land, and in all the 'forests', whether wooded or not, husbandry and farming were restricted in favour of the chase. Here the countryfolk had to suffer the depredations of hunter and hunted alike. One way and another, so many thick woods remained even in the sixteenth century, that countrymen in various parts delighted in vying with each other in boasts of how far their local squirrels could travel by leaping from tree to tree.

Yet woodland and champion were not always neatly divided

the one from the other. Nor did all the woods stand on heavy, wet, vale lands. In parts of all the downlands, and especially in the North Downs and the Chiltern Hills, where the chalk had disintegrated into clays studded with flints, and where the tall beech woods raised their heads, the same kinds of woody close were to be found as in the wood-pasture lands, and yet were as much the domain of the sheep as were the smoothest downs, for they all stood on the same chalk base, and these enclosed districts, too, had their 'Russet lawns, and fallows grey, Where the nibbling sheep do stray'. And conversely, many of the heavy lands of the Midlands, which have since been enclosed into fatting grounds for sheep and cattle, were for centuries cultivated in naked expanses of ploughland. These 'fielden' districts were, so to speak, torn from the body of the woodland and forcibly annexed to the champion.

Sheep-and-Corn Husbandry

In all the downlands, the champion and the fielden, in all save the strictly wood-pasture districts, the sheepfold was the sheet-anchor and mainstay of husbandry. The same flocks that were driven each morning to feed on the downs, wolds, hills, heaths, commons, and pastures, were brought back to the ploughland at night to be folded behind hurdles, in small and crowded pens, so that they would deposit there the residues resulting from their day's nibbling, chewing and drinking. The sheep were thus used as four-footed muckspreaders, or, rather, as mobile combinations of fertilizer manufacturers, distributors and spreaders, fetching their own raw materials and processing them, and delivering and applying their products. This meant, incidentally, that one part of the farmland was continually being robbed in order to enrich the rest, and that everything was sacrificed to corn-growing. The whole farm was laid out and run to suit the sheep, but only on the strict understanding that they devoted themselves to ferti-lizing the land for corn and grain.

So essential were sheep for the growing of corn that Hugh Latimer, the famous bishop, took it for granted in one of his sermons that 'A ploughland must have sheep; yea, they must

have sheep to help fat the ground; for if they have no sheep
to help fat the ground, they shall have but bare corn and thin'.
In the days before chemical fertilizers, this now almost forgotten
fact was one of the great assumptions on which English people
based their lives. It permeated their thoughts and their poetry.
In Sir Walter Raleigh's *The Nymph's Reply*, 'Time drives the
flocks from field to fold'. Milton constantly recurs to this theme.
When Adam opened his eyes, he 'beheld a field, Part arable and
tilth, whereon were sheaves new-reap'd; The other part sheepwalks and folds'. The poet sees 'The folded flocks penn'd in
their wattled cotes' and watches 'where shepherds pen their
flocks at eve, In hurdled cotes amid the field secure'. He sets
the scene when 'the chewing flocks Had ta'en their supper on
the savoury herb, Of knot-grass dew-besprent, and were in fold'.
To Lycidas he sings,

> For we were nursed upon the self-same hill,
> Fed the same flock, by fountain, shade or rill,
> Together both, ere the high lawns appear'd
> Under the opening eye-lids of the morn,
> We drove afield, and both together heard
> What time the grey fly winds her sultry horn,
> Battening our flocks with the fresh dews of night,
> Oft till the star that rose at evening bright.

And this was 'The star', as he explains in *Comus*, 'that bids the
shepherd fold'. Feeding by day and folding by night gave the
rustic world its rhythm.

The Meadowlands

To keep sheep for the fold, horses for the plough and cows for
the pail, the husbandman needed grass. But grass stopped growing in the winter months, so that the summer growth had partly
to be preserved for the winter, in the form of hay. Without hay
there could be no livestock, and therefore little corn, and most
people would starve. True, straw could be fed to the stock in
winter and was, with a bit of luck, enough to keep them just
alive, but without the hay there could have been little or no

straw crop in the first instance. It is true, too, that tares (*plate 5*) were grown in parts of the fallows, and served then as clover crops do now, so that some tare-hay could be saved; but tares could only be grown if the land were well manured, and without grass-hay there would have been precious little manure for growing tares. Life thus depended heavily on supplies of grass-hay. It was only when the farmers had their hay cut and dried that the future of civilization was secured.

Nearly all the hay, then, came from grass, and grass in the way farmers use the word means grass plus the other herbs, usually and naturally, found growing with it. Just as when we mow our lawns, we cut some plants that a botanist would not dignify with the name of grass, so the swathes made by the scythe included much that was grass only in common speech. No matter, the farmers made hay of it all.

This hay could be made either from dry, upland meadows or from wet, bottom ones. The upland meadows were really the richest parts of the ordinary grasslands, which could be laid to hay from time to time. Before the start of the agricultural revolution, there was not much upland meadow, because livestock could not be kept in sufficient numbers to enrich the grasslands enough to allow them, as a rule, to be mown and grazed in any rotation. Thus nearly all the hay came from permanent, wet meadows set aside for this especial purpose. They could be mown down every year and still leave an aftermath for the animals to feed on. The same stream watered both beasts and grass. As the great rains filled and overflowed the rivers and bournes, their valleys or plains were flooded. If the flood-waters could not get away, the ground was reduced to a marsh; but if they could drain off after a time, they left behind lush, green grass. When this had been mown a few times, so encouraging the early grasses and cutting down the later ones before they seeded, good meadowland resulted. Such wet meadows gave about three times as much hay an acre as the dry and upland ones, and gave it not just occasionally, but year in and year out. But they were severely limited in their extent. They were the eyes of the land, like waterholes in the bush and artesian wells in the outback.

No farmstead, no village could be built unless hard by them. They were much prized, but also scarce.

There was thus every incentive to try to extend these wet meadows. One way of doing this was by draining the riverside marshes by means of trenches and ditches; but this was not always possible. Another way of extending the area of meadow was by damming up the stream and forcing it along trenches and channels to water and irrigate land that would not otherwise have been flooded. Numerous artificial watermeadows were made in this way in the Middle Ages, both in river valleys, where the task was relatively easy, and on the sides of hills, where artificial rills or leats were led along the contours to supply mill-ponds and watering-pools and at the same time to carry the water to a trench overlooking the valley. Spilling over the brim of this trench, the water would then run down and irrigate the slopes. In these ways the meadows were manured as well as watered, and the old writers highly commended 'water that cometh out of a town from every man's midden or dunghill', 'fat rivers and gulfs of water participating of a slimy and muddy substance . . . from town ditches, sewers, ways, streets, tilths'.

The Marshes

Along the coasts much could be done both to improve the land and to win more of it from the sea. The action of strong tides cast up banks of silt and sand, and when these had been built up above the ordinary tide level, glasswort, samphire and similar plants soon took root and consolidated the land thus formed, leaving it open to invasion by cotton-grass, common saltmarsh grass and other species suited to those ever ready friends of the farmer, the ubiquitous sheep. By grazing the coarse swards of these saltings, the sheep improved them and made them firmer, and their masters kept out the highest tides by building walls of clay, chalk rubble and timber. Later the walls were faced on the seaward side with a 'needlework' of bramble and thorn faggots secured to a wooden frame. Finally, stone or brick facings might be laid. Outside the walls, the tides might perhaps repeat their work of casting up banks. Inside, the saltmarsh that had been 'inned' from the sea was converted into fresh marsh, for the walls that shut out the tides also shut in the waters flowing from inland. To drain this fresh marsh the improvers therefore directed the numerous creeks, that now vainly sought the sea, into and along square troughs and through the walls to sluice-doors, where they made their exit. These sluices were constructed in such a way that they opened under the pressure of the fresh waters when the salt sea had ebbed and were forced shut again by the pressure of the high tide. For this reason the doors were popularly known as 'tankard-lids'. Thus were created both Wallasey in the west and Wallasea in the east.

In their natural state many parts of the interior of England were marshes of little or no use to the inhabitants. They were called fens in eastern England, mosses in the north-west, and moors in the south-west, but were all much the same. As the vegetation in them died and was buried under numberless layers of new growth, great beds of peat were formed in many of these marshes, giving a ready supply of fuel to the people round about. These tracts were often veritable bogs, and large parts of England must at one time have looked much like the boggy districts of Ireland, with their flat expanses, their wraiths of mist, and their stacks of cut peat. Indeed, it is widely believed that the broads of Norfolk and Suffolk were formed in the Middle Ages by the continual cutting of peat that lowered the level and invited flooding at the first mischance. Other fens, however, were being drained and improved from very early times by means of trenches, sewers and embankments. This was especially so in the great fens of the eastern counties (*plate 15*). Long before the sixteenth century the men of those parts had made the greater part of these marshes dry enough to be able to get plenty of rough grazing and coarse hay from them in the summer months. As they put it, the fens were now largely good 'summer-ground'. And occasionally, in the dryer seasons, in the best and highest parts, the farmers could even grow little plots of oats. The best drained district of all was Marshland in Norfolk (*plate 14*). A good deal of land here could be cultivated through-out the year—it was 'winterground'. Yet elsewhere, notably around Crowland, there were still not a few 'fishing fields', which were hardly better than broads. All these fenny districts abounded in fish and wild fowl, especially ducks and eels. Ely did not get its name for nothing and was far from having the only 'eely' thereabouts.

The Path of the Plough

When all is said and done, what most tamed the wilderness was the tilling of the soil. Generation after generation of thousands and thousands of ploughmen launched endless waves of assault on nature along two fronts, one the broadest possible, the other somewhat narrower. On the first and broadest front, the ploughs were engaged only in the temporary cultivation of small plots of land selected from the wilderness. These plots were cleared and tilled for corn until the harvest no longer returned the seed. Then they were allowed to revert to the wild and new plots were taken in to replace them. Much later on, centuries afterwards, this shifting cultivation was largely, but by no means entirely, superseded by permanent cultivation. Crops were now grown on the land reserved always, and exclusively, for this purpose. It was tilled every year without fail.

Before the temporary plots in shifting cultivation could possibly be tilled, they had to be cleared. Trees and bushes were felled and grubbed up. Coarse swards were pared off and burned in heaps and their ashes mixed with the soil. Boulders were removed out of the plough's way and stones and other underground obstructions picked out by hand. Then the crops sown in the plot needed some protection from the denizens of the surrounding wilderness, and this was often best provided by dry stone walls or earthen mounds, and then the rubble cleared away could be conveniently used as foundations for these. Finally, when the last crop had been sown, the mark of the plough, as we shall see, was often left upon the surface of the soil. The plot might be allowed to revert to the wild for twenty years or more, but even this wilderness was never quite the same again.

In its time, the introduction of permanent cultivation, which was largely the work of the Anglo-Saxons, had amounted to a veritable economic revolution. It enormously economized in the use of land. Although the yields per acre of tillage might often be less than in temporary cultivation, the total yields of a given amount of available farmland were mightily increased and multiplied, allowing a much denser population than before. This invention of permanent cultivation was signalled by the novel distinctions now made between permanent tillage, which was called 'arable', and permanent grassland, which was known as 'pasture', or as 'pasture and meadow' if occasionally laid for hay. These two classes of land, like the permanent woods also, were kept quite separate and distinct. 'Arable' was rarely laid down for 'pasture' or 'pasture' ploughed up for 'arable', and even then only with the intention of extending the area either of permanent tillage or of permanent grass. Much of the land was thus bound to a perpetual tillage.

However, the poorer lands lent themselves neither to permanent tillage nor to permanent grass. They were too weak to bear corn in alternate years or to stand always in grass. Thus, even when permanent cultivation had become generally adopted as the ordinary system, large areas in some parts long continued to be cultivated only temporarily and afterwards left to gather heart again as best they could. Indeed, some land has never progressed beyond this. Thin and infertile soils such as were found in and about the Pennine hills and poor heaths like the one at Bagshot could never be tilled year in and year out. And, even if all the land had been strong enough for permanent tillage, it could not all have been tilled permanently, for then there would have been nowhere to feed the flocks needed to fertilize the tillage.

Even the best land could be subjected permanently to the plough only by continual labour and expense. After one or two or sometimes a few more crops, the land had to be left unsown for six, twelve or eighteen months, or even for two years, so that the opportunity might be taken of restoring its fertility. Nor would as much as two years be anywhere near long enough for the land to recover heart of itself. Instead, the husbandmen had perforce to fallow the land and use all his art to make it fertile. In soils that were too light and dry to work without their being blown away on any wind that might spring up, the fallow field was left quite still and undisturbed. Cattle and folded flocks of sheep were put into it, but it was left unbroken by the plough until the preparing of a seed-bed for the next crop could no longer be delayed. Elsewhere, and generally, the fallow was stirred and turned over from time to time, the weeds buried, farmyard and other manure ploughed in, and the soil aerated and made crumbly both by the plough itself and by weathering down in sun, frost, wind and rain. Bearing in mind that a 'sull' was a plough, and that 'soil' signified manure, we can understand the old saying, 'The sun and the sull are some husbandmen's soil'. Of course, the longer the fallow, the more refreshed and reinvigorated was the land. Hence the old rhyme,

> The greedy villager likes best that mould,
> Which twice hath left the sun and twice the cold

No matter whether stirred or left still, the fallow land had always to be heavily mucked and manured. Farmyard manure was taken out to it in tumbrels or dung-pots, which were usually tip-carts, but in some hilly districts simply panniers with drop-bottoms slung across ponies or pack-horses. The manure thus heaped was then spread and ploughed in. The obvious thing to do was to start mucking the fields nearest the farmyard and then work gradually farther and farther afield, but avoiding steep hills and other places difficult to access, for there could never be enough farmyard manure for the whole farm, and the parts that were hardest to muck were sure to be the ones easiest to fold. The sheep made light of the hills and, since they spent their days in outlying pastures, had the least way to go to the fields that lay at the greatest distance from the farmstead.

Permanent tillage wrought a great and permanent change in the countryside. Nature was expelled bell, book and candle. Scarcely a blade of grass escaped the folded sheep, or a weed the plough, or a root the tines of the harrows and forks. All was left clean for corn and grain. And then, if weeds later invaded the crop, hand-weeders went to work and pulled them up by the roots. The wilderness was not just temporarily overridden; it was permanently subjugated.

Then vast tracts of ploughland met the eye. The land John Aubrey knew as a boy 'was anciently a delicate Campania— all ploughed fields', with only a few small closes of grass around the farmhouses and cottages. The countryside was bare and naked, almost without hedges or trees, so much so that the inhabitants could not find so much as a few sticks to make a fire with. In these places, Aubrey tells us, 'where fuel is scarce, the poor people do strew straw in the barton, on which the cows do dung, and then they clap it against the stone walls to dry for fuel'. Amongst other places, this was common practice in the uplands of Lincolnshire. Hence the old saw, 'Lincolnshire, where the pig shits soap and the cow shits fire!', the former providing soft soap and the latter fuel. To find such practices nowadays one would have to travel to India or Peru. And to find such a countryside one would have to penetrate the interior of Syria, where now, as then in many parts of England, the eye is met by 'vast, naked plains, without trees or hedges, where almost geometrically regular fields stretch as far as the eye can see; a harlequin's doublet, with the dominant colours changing with the seasons: red, brown or grey after the first rains of autumn, when the plough is everywhere turning over fresh soil; light green in early winter with the first push of the wheat and rye; deep green in spring as the corn sprouts, except for the fallows and their motley of wild flowers; straw-coloured when the corn begins to ripen; but tawny-grey during late summer, when the fallows and stubbles merge into the same dusty uniformity.' (Jacques Weulersse)

The Art of Ploughing

Exactly how the countryside became patterned and grained by the plough depended to a great extent on the system of ploughing adopted. Some thin and free-draining soils were tilled with a light plough or drag, not unlike the *araire* or scratch-plough used in Mediterranean lands. These drag-ploughs merely tore up the

surface of the soil without in the least turning it over. In order
to get a decent tilth, the ploughmen had to work first in one
direction and then at right angles to it, ploughing and cross-
ploughing. This meant, first, that the surface of the land was
little altered in the ploughing, and, secondly, that it was convenient to have the fields more or less square, so that the distance
travelled in cross-ploughing was much the same as in ploughing
and wastefully short journeys were avoided. But some of these
soils needed paring and burning before cropping, and all had
to be defended when in corn, so that they were commonly
surrounded by a mound or wall of rubble covered with mud
and overgrown with grass. In this way the field plots themselves
have often been preserved as permanent monuments. Many of
them may still be seen in the heaths, downs and hills, either by
the naked eye or in aerial photographs. These fields are, for no
very good reason, called 'Celtic' or 'iron-age', and are marked
as 'Celtic' in Ordnance survey maps, but it hardly needs to be said
that we rarely have any historical evidence showing when they
were first cultivated, though we do know that crops continued
to be grown in them until relatively recent times.

Fig. 2. Turning over the furrow slice. A slice is being turned over by the
plough and laid alongside previous ones.

All the heavier and deeper soils were ploughed with a sull
or heavy plough in the ridge-and-furrow system. In this, the
land was ploughed in ridges composed of furrow slices laid side
by side. These slices were cut first vertically by the coulter and
then horizontally by the share. They were then turned over by
the mould-board and stacked side by side one against the other,
as shown in the following figures. These furrow slices could be

Fig. 3.   Profile of rectangular furrow slices. The broken line indicates the
original level of the ground.

cut in one of three main forms: rectangular, crested, or wide
(*figures 2, 3, 4, 5*). Crested furrows were used in winter ploughing and fallowing, for they exposed a larger surface to the elements
and so facilitated weathering down. Wide furrows were favoured
when a more even surface was required. A completed bed of
furrow slices made up what was called a stitch, butt, loon, or,
more usually and expressively, a ridge, for it was raised slightly

Fig. 4.   Profile of crested furrow slices. The broken line indicates the original
level of the ground.

above the former level of the surface. The narrow strip of land
between two ridges was called a rein or open furrow or simply
a furrow. Since the water draining through and under the
furrow slices of the ridge found its way into the channel formed
by the open furrows, these were, if necessary, 'made up' by
ploughing a last 'mould' or 'hind-end' furrow to deepen and
round off the open furrow and so convert it into a 'water-

Fig. 5.   Profile of wide or broad furrow slices. The broken line indicates the
original level of the ground.

furrow' along which the superfluous water could readily flow
(*figures 6, 7, 8*).

Ridges and furrows were sometimes ploughed to lie north and
south so they could enjoy the sun equally throughout the day;
but the overriding consideration, except upon steep hillsides, was

to make them follow the slope of the ground and allow the water to flow away more freely. The width of the ridge, and therefore the frequency of the intervening open or water-furrows, and the profiles of both, were designed to give the best possible surface drainage (*plate 1*).

Fig. 6. Profile of completed water-furrow showing rectangular furrow slices of adjacent ridges with the two mould or hind-end furrows ploughed from the open furrow and laid against the flanks of the ridges. The upper broken line indicates the original level of the ground. The lower broken line indicates the level of the open furrow before the mould furrows were ploughed from it.

When a piece of land was ploughed ridge-and-furrow for the first time, the initial furrow had to be drawn across it by reference to guides or landmarks, which were usually supplied by placing aligned poles at either end. In subsequent ploughings this alignment was normally unnecessary and the ploughman simply took his cue from the ridges and furrows discernible on the ground.

The ploughman went right across the land, laying a furrow slice one way. Then he turned about and came back, laying another furrow slice over against the first one, and so forming

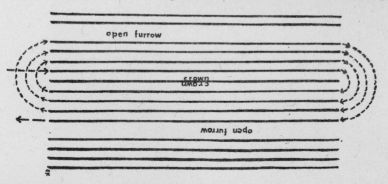

Fig. 7. Diagram showing the direction taken by the plough in forming a ridge.

a crown from the two of them. After this, he went on ploughing round and round the crown until the consequent ridge reached the required width. Since each furrow slice was cut out to the depth required and then turned right over by the plough, cross-ploughing was quite unnecessary. As a result of this system of ploughing, the ridges, like the furrow slices of which they were composed, were a furrow long, or, in other words, a natural furlong, but much less in breadth (*figure 7*).

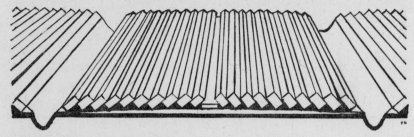

Fig. 8.   The ridge twice elevated, showing mould furrows, water-furrows, and pronounced ridge-and-furrow effect.

When the time came round to plough the same land again, it could, if wanted, be retained in ridges of the same slight elevation formerly set up, simply by ploughing crown-and-furrow. By this process the old open furrows became the crowns of the new ridges, and the old crowns the new open furrows, as each old ridge was split or slit down the middle and the furrow slices thrown the opposite way from before. Crown-and-furrow ploughing was practised in order to keep the land more or less level, very high ridges not being needed where the soil was relatively dry and absorbent, for example, in the chalk downlands. Here William Cobbett found 'the most delightful country in the world, no ditches, no water-furrows, no drains, hardly any hedges, no dirt or mire even in the wettest seasons of the year'. In such dry country, indeed, the ridges could often be coupled or ploughed two-in-and-two out. In coupling or casting, all the furrow slices of a whole ridge were laid over in one direction, while those of the next ridge were all laid in the opposite one, in such a way that two ridges were made into one and the number of open furrows was halved. In two-in-and-two-out ploughing, the furrow slices or two whole and adjacent ridges were all laid over in the one direction, and those of the next two ridges in the opposite one. One ridge was thus made out of four and the open furrows correspondingly reduced.

But in heavier, wetter and more retentive land, this slight elevation was not usually sufficient for the purposes of surface drainage. Therefore the second and third ploughings were made just the same as the first, so that the ridges that had been elevated once were now raised a second and a third time. This amounted to ploughing the land out of the water and had the obvious advantage of saving the corn on the ridges in an exceptionally wet year and sparing that in and near the water-furrows in an unusually dry one. This ploughing of high ridges or high-backs was as old as the hills. Walter of Henley, the thirteenth-century writer, advised, 'When your lands are sown, let the marshy and damp ground be well ridged, and the water made to run, so that the ground may be freed from water.' One result of elevating the ridges twice or thrice was to make them high, steep, and ridged at the crown (*figure 8, plate 1*). Of course, land that had been twice or thrice elevated could easily be brought down again as required. The ridges could be slit down the middle and the furrow slices returned to their former level.

Land was thrown into high ridges because it was wet and retentive and the water could have no other riddance. Often this was a natural characteristic of the soil and not to be altered by any amount of improvement. This is why the stiffest lands in eastern England are still ploughed in narrow, elevated ridges. But sometimes the land was so retentive and wet not only on account of its nature but also because it was kept in permanent tillage and half-starved of humus. As grass was never allowed to take root in it, and not much vegetable matter was ploughed back in, the soil was far less absorbent than it might have been. In later times, in the self-same places, where corn was alternated with grass, it proved unnecessary to elevate the ridges as much as before, because the humus or 'turf' in the land made it absorb water better. This was explained to William Marshall, the great

C

agricultural writer, by old George Barwell, when asked why he made such high ridges, in these words:

'Yea, Sur, we mun lie 'em up, a-thissen, or we canno get onny wheat. An us lie 'em flat o' th' top, th' first pash of rain runs 'em into lakes, and sets the crop. It hen been tried a many time; but it wunno do. . . . Yea, yea, Sur, when they ha'gotten some turf in 'em, they wunno run, a-thaten; but here we fallow, fallow, fallow, every three year, till they runnen like lime welly; and if they dunno lien up sharp, we canno get onny wheat, skant.'

(*Mun = must; a-thissen = as this one; a-thaten = as that one; onny = any; hen = have; wunno = will not; welly means verily; and skant scarcely. Yea, of course, was pronounced as in America and East Anglia nowadays.*)

As long as heavy lands were kept in permanent tillage, high ridges were the order of the day and much of the countryside was corrugated, often remarkably so, and with some strange and comical results. It is said, for example, that at the battle of Naseby, high ridges and water-furrows served as a ready-made complex of trenches. The tale is told of horse-riders who stayed out of sight by keeping to the water-furrows. Perhaps the best of many such stories is the one of the farmer who lent some of his plough-horses to a neighbour. On going over to find out how his friend was getting on with his ploughing, he was surprised to see no teams at work, where he had expected five or six. The explanation was, 'they were making up their furrows, and were wholly hid, by the ridges, from his sight'.

Anyone who has travelled by train through the Midlands or other districts with heavy, wet soils, will have noticed how ridge-and-furrow ploughing has marked the landscape. Much of this remaining corrugation was in fact formed at a time when the land had already been converted from permanent tillage and was being alternated between corn and grass. For this reason, many of the ridges are not very high. But in some places they may still be found as they were twice and thrice elevated, as they were ploughed in bygone ages. Incidentally, it should perhaps be pointed out that the elevated ridges we so often see today were largely ploughed in enclosed fields. There is no truth in the idea that the ridges show the extent of the old common fields (*plate 1*).

Needless to say, ridge-and-furrow ploughing was not confined to fields of permanent tillage. The temporary tillage plots of shifting cultivation were often ploughed ridge-and-furrow, and this enabled men to know for certain that some plots had been ploughed at some time in the past. In the uplands of the West Country, in Devon and Cornwall, where temporary cultivation was the general rule, vast areas became covered with the characteristically narrow ridges ploughed there for wheat and winter corn.

However, ridge and furrow by themselves could hardly provide most fields with anything like complete surface drainage, for the water-furrows alone would only have taken water from the centre of the field in order to drown its sides. The water draining off had to be carried from the water-furrows and over the headlands, where the plough had been turned round, by means of drains and gutters, or drawn off to the side by cross-gutters. These gutters could be made with a trenching spade or a hand trenching-plough, but these were mostly useful for putting the finishing touches to work carried out by the trench-plough, properly so called. This was a huge piece of equipment that had to be drawn by a team of up to a score of horses or nine yoke of oxen led by two pairs of horses. A trench-plough had two coulters, a flat share, and a huge mould-board, enabling it to cut a trench one foot deep, a foot wide at the bottom and eighteen inches at the top, and to throw out the earth in a single giant slice. In many places, too, underdrainage was needed in addition to everything else. A trench was cut in the impervious base below the soil and drains constructed of bushes, turves, stones, cinders, or alderwood pipes.

Terraces and Linchets

We have seen that ridges and furrows usually followed the slope of the land. But on the steep sides of cultivable hills, it was better practice to plough along the line of the contours. This impeded the headlong fall of rainwaters and the erosion of the soil they would have caused, and enabled advantage to be taken of the inevitable creeping of the soil downhill. Along the contours of many hillsides, then, the tillage was laid out in terraces, which had been ploughed out of the hillside, though sometimes with the assistance of some spade-work. These terraces were divided the one from the other by greensward 'walls', 'linches', 'linchards' or 'linchets', which had likewise been made up partly by spade and pick in some instances.

Ordnance survey maps mark these terraces as 'strip lynchets' and they have attracted a good deal of attention from time to time and have occasionally been explained in various amusing ways. Some bright imaginations have even believed them to be running tracks laid down by the ancients for some series of prehistoric games. More realistic explanations are to be found, however, in the writings of knowledgeable farmers. A. G. Street describes the traces of such contour ploughing he found in Ditchampton Farm, and such terraces may readily be seen in various parts of England, including, amongst other places, Salisbury Plain, the Marlborough Downs, the Craven district and the Cotswold and Chiltern hills (*plates 2, 17*). Cobbett tells us, 'I saw, on my way through the down countries, hundreds of acres of ploughed land in shelves'. Not long before William Marshall had remarked,

'The artificial surface which meets the eye in different parts of these hills, forcibly arrests the attention. It occurs on the steeper slopes, which are formed into stages or platforms, with grassy steeps, provincially "linchets", between them. . . . The stages or platforms are equally commodious for implements of tillage, as for carriages; besides retaining moisture better than sloping surfaces; while the grassy steeps, between the arable stages, afford no inconsiderable supply of herbage; on which horses are teddered, or tended, while corn is in the ground; and which gives pasturage to sheep at other seasons. This sort of artificial surface is common in different parts of the island.'

Here, then, was yet another way in which the English countryside was fashioned by the hand of man.

Farm Implements

The ploughs and other instruments that generations of English-men have used to make the English countryside have always been designed for specific uses. Ploughs were designed and made according to what had to be ploughed, and as soils, situations and requirements varied greatly, so did the ploughs. As John Worlidge of Petersfield once said,

'There is a very great difference in ploughs, that there is scarce any sure rule for the making of them—and every country, yes, almost every county, differs not only in the ploughs, but even in every part of them. Ploughs do not only differ according to the several customs of several places, but also as the lands do differ in strength or weakness or the different nature of the soil.'

Thus there were wheel-ploughs, and ploughs without wheels, ploughs with a foot for sliding over sticky land, and swing ploughs that could hold themselves down in heavy soil; fen-ploughs with disc-coulters and broad-finned shares, turn-wrest ploughs for hillsides, light ploughs for sandy soils, drag-ploughs for the thin ones, trenching ploughs for drains, and breast-ploughs for pushing to pare off the turf. It followed, too, that the farmer who was anybody needed to have more than one kind of plough and each plough with more than one set of irons, so that he could deal appropriately with all his different cultivations, like fallowing, breaking up grass or stubbles, or preparing fine tilths, and in all his different types of land (*figure 9*). Similarly, there were various kinds of stone, wooden, and iron rollers, of light and heavy harrows, and of carts, farm wains and everything else.

The Fruits of the Earth

This man-made countryside was draped with a wide variety of crops, every strain of which had been selected and bred for special purposes over a long period of years and so was as artificial as the countryside itself. There were rivet or cone wheats for cold, retentive and rank soil, and bread wheats, some bearded, some nott (unbearded), for ordinary crops. These were

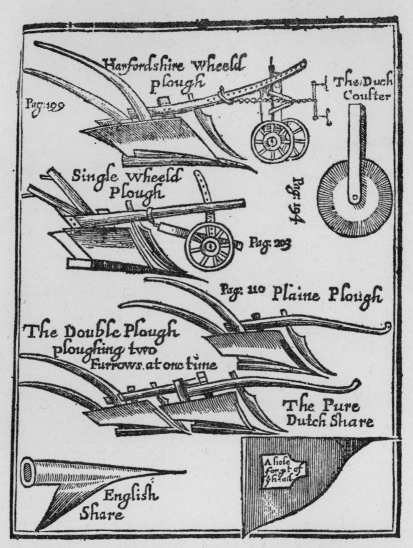

Fig. 9.   English ploughs 1652. These drawings illustrate Walter Blith's *English Improver Improved*. The 'Hartfordshire' (Hertfordshire) plough was used in the Chiltern and Chalk Countries, the plain plough in the Midland Plain and similar situations. The Dutch coulter and Dutch share were for drained fenlands. The double plough was then a relatively new invention. (British Museum.)

all winter wheats. Spring varieties did exist, but were not often grown. Conversely, spring barleys were much more usual than winter ones. Bigg, or 'beer', the chief variety of winter barley, was hardly met with outside the northerly parts of England (*plate 3*). As for the spring barleys, some were late-ripening, some middle-ripening, and some were rathe-ripe or hotspur varieties. Rye, too, was known in both winter and spring types, but it was the winter ones that were most often sown, and then either as a separate crop or in a mixture or maslin with wheat. There were naked oats, which made porridge without any milling, black oats and 'skegs' for poor lands, and red, white and reed oats for good ones (*plate 4*). Then there were grey or field peas in great variety, including hotspurs; horse, field or tick beans, with some winter varieties as well as many spring ones; and both winter and spring vetches and tares (*plate 5*). Add to these rape or cole-seed for growing in marshy lands (*plate 7*), buckwheat for poultry-feed (*plate 6*), mustard for smothering the weeds, woad for dyestuffs (*plate 8*), saffron for condiments (*plate 9*), flax and hemp for linens and sackcloths, and many other minor crops. As for the grasslands, they were replete with virtually every worthwhile species of 'grass', including old common sainfoin, perennial rye-grass, cat's tail (timothy), and nearly all the clovers and vetches. A hundred and one plants of as many shades of green coloured the farmers' fields and the countryside of England.

Chapter Two

THE COUNTRYMEN

The Service-tenancy System

Modern British agriculture is a business conducted by farmers, many of whom have their land on a lease or tenancy from a landowner, who in some instances is a member of an old county family or of the nobility. In their turn many of these farmers employ farm workers of various kinds and pay them wages, mainly in money, but often partly in fringe benefits like 'tied' cottages at nominal rents or the chance to buy farm produce at cut prices. If we hark back to Roman and early Anglo-Saxon times, however, we shall find matters arranged quite differently. Then much of the land belonged to great magnates who were also slave-owners. They put their slaves to work in the fields and either consumed or sold all that these wretched people produced, except only what little was required to feed, clothe and shelter them in the roughest and cheapest way that would keep them fit to work as ordered.

In the Middle Ages, and to a large extent still in the sixteenth century, a third and quite distinct method of running agriculture was adopted. This was the service-tenancy system. Under this, the tenant, in return for the holding on which he made his own living, gave his services to its owner. These services commonly included so many days' work or a number of specific tasks to be performed on land that the lord or owner kept in his own hands for his own use. Sometimes, however, money or produce was paid instead of labour, or the dues or rents were made up of mixed labour, produce and cash. These services did not have to be given by the tenant in person. He could get someone else to deputise for him. But even then the charge fell on the tenant. Service-tenancies something like this are occasionally found nowadays, as when staff cottages are let in return for domestic help. But in order to grasp what kind of society the Elizabethans were heir to, we must imagine a world where service tenancies were no rarity but the all-pervading system. A society in which most people were service-tenants of one kind or another seems strange to us now, but it had this in common with our system, that it involved a good deal of give and take. The lord got the service he needed to keep up his position in the world and his service-tenant got his dearest wish, which was to have a piece of land he could call his own.

One way the service-tenancy system had come about was this. The harsh and unnatural conditions in which slaves had been kept meant they could not raise proper families and keep up their own numbers. Consequently the very existence of slavery depended on more or less regular supplies of fresh slaves being captured. But as the Roman armies eventually became bogged down in the static defence of over-extended frontiers, and again when the Anglo-Saxons had settled down peacefully in England, the number of captives for sale as slaves fell sharply. In consequence, slaves came into short supply and their price shot up. What with the high price of slaves and the disruption of trade that accompanied the decline and break-up of the Roman empire, the slave-owner on his plantation was caught in a squeeze between rising costs and falling prices. Unlike a modern employer, he could not just lay some men off when business was slack. He still had to keep his slaves or lose what he had paid out for them. The only thing a slave-owner could do, then, was to tell his slaves to shift for themselves as best they could, though on no account to leave the estate. This meant the owner had to allow his slaves to live in their own cabins or huts and to marry and set up house for themselves. He had also to allot them pieces of land on which they could grow their own food and fend for themselves and their families. But they still had to work several days a week for their owner on the land he kept to himself to provide for his own housekeeping. These hutted slaves now kept up their own numbers, so their owner had no need to buy replacements. They also provided both their own subsistence and that of their lord and master, and this on a more lavish scale, for the slaves now had an incentive to work, at least when they were working to keep themselves.

Another way service-tenancies were set up was when the owners of newly-acquired estates and lands, in preference to buying slaves or enslaving the previous occupants, invited colonists to settle on them in return for services to be rendered. Such settlers could equally well be recruited from amongst the conquered Welsh or the poor and landless amongst the con- quering English. The advantage of taking such settlers was that they worked in a willing spirit and were more productive than even the best and cheapest of slaves could be made. Many men were eager to become service-tenants. Hitherto perfectly free and independent peasants who had been impoverished by bad harvests, warfare or some other disaster were only too willing to surrender their land to a powerful lord, in return for the mere use of it and a supply of corn, seed and livestock to tide them over. In a not altogether dissimilar way, some masterless freemen put themselves and their lands under a lord's protection and became his henchmen purely and simply for the sake of self-preservation in times of war and lawlessness.

The Feudal System

Once a slave had been hutted and given an allotment of land, he was no longer a slave in the full meaning of the word. Looked at from the purely economic point of view, he was no longer a slave at all, but a service-tenant, and his master was no longer a slave-owner but a lord over dependent peasants. To this new reality the laws and customs were then made to conform, in various ways and degrees. Many owners manumitted their slaves, making them legally freed men. Anglo-Saxon lords and ladies frequently emancipated by their wills the people they had owned in life. Sometimes the same will bequeathed emancipation and confirmed existing service-tenancy arrangements by saying, for instance, 'All my men are to be free, and each is to have his homestead and his cow and his corn for food'. The land laws were similarly adapted. Under the circumstances there could be no private ownership of land in the strict, full and complete meaning of the term. No one exactly owned the service-tenants' allotments. The tenants had their property in them, since custom came to allow them the use of the land and buildings; and the lord had his property in them, for he was the owner of the dues and services arising from them, as well as the residuary owner of the allotment should it be left untenanted. And going up the social scale, the whole of the kingdom was constructed out of an interlocking succession of similar service-tenancies. As John Aubrey said, 'The government was like a nest of boxes, for copyholders [who were called villeins] held of the lords of the manor, who held of a superior lord, who perhaps held of another superior lord or duke, who held of the king'.

This is often called the 'feudal system'. In the higher ranks of society men held their land by honourable service-tenancies, fees or feus, as, for example, by knight-service. In the lower ranks men held base fees by agricultural and other base services. But whether he served with the plough or with the sword, a man did so by virtue of the possession of a fee that made him a cog on the wheels of feudal society. And even the base tenants, though bound to perform all their dues and services, were ordinarily free in all other respects.

Serfs or Bondmen

In point of fact, a small minority of the population was not free at all. This was a remnant of the slaves, some of whom had not yet been freed. Most of these no longer functioned as slaves, but as service-tenants, even though they were still legally slaves. When the Domesday Book was made in 1086, only about one person in ten was a slave, called *servus* in Latin and 'bondman' in later English. (The word 'serf' employed by Continental writers means just the same again.) In the course of centuries, and especially after Henry VIII dissolved the monasteries, which were great slave-owners, many bondmen bought their freedom. But bondage, slavery, or serfdom, only finally disappeared in the early seventeenth century, when neither the law courts nor anyone else would be bothered with it any longer. In the meantime, however, these unfortunate bondmen passed their slavery down from father and mother to children, and could be bought and sold and traded in just like any other livestock. They might hold goods and chattels, including land, but only on sufferance of their lords and owners, who could take them back any time they wanted. Bondmen might go and live away from their owner's land, but only under licence and subject to payments. If they fled, their owners could pursue and retrieve them. Even in the sixteenth century, the Duke of Norfolk is found making the lord mayor of Norwich give up one of his bondmen who was absent without leave. In 1552 the lord of Enford manor had a list drawn up of 'Bondmen, otherwise called due men' who 'are to be seized and put to fines or as the lord pleases.' A blind widowwoman with six young children 'at this present time yet going a-gooding, which is piteous and heavy to see', is turned out of house and holding at a moment's notice. An abbot claps one of his bondmen in irons and throws him into a dungeon.

Customary Services

Bondmen were an oppressed class, but they were a small and decreasing minority. The overwhelming majority of base service-tenants were freemen and bound only to perform their dues and services, which varied greatly from place to place and from time to time. Where the lord had little need of labour on the demesne lands he kept in his own hands, the services often consisted mainly of paying fixed sums of money by way of rent. Where the lord used his demesnes for corn growing, the services were largely in field-labour, called customary works. Sometimes the service was chiefly giving the lord corn or some other rent in kind. Most frequently, however, the tenant owed a mixed bag of services that included rent in kind, in money and in the form of labour services. For their ordinary week-work, the tenants would have to go with their teams and ploughs to till the lord's ground, sow his corn and reap his harvest. By the sixteenth century, this heavy load of week-work had largely been commuted into money rent, and the lords or their farmers made much more use of wage-labour, but the lighter harvest or 'boon' work often continued as before, because at harvest and certain other times every available hand was needed.

A not altogether untypical example of the set of services that might be owed is drawn from Netherhampton, in the Chalk Country, in 1567. Each of the twenty tenants with a standard holding paying £1 rent a year,

'shall at the feast of St Michael the Archangel or at any time about that season, upon a lawful warning, ear [plough] four halves [half-acres] and edge [harrow] the same. And the said tenants shall wash and shear the whole flock of sheep going upon the farm or manor of Washern. Also the said tenants and every of them shall mow one acre in Woodmiln Mead and make it ready for the cart to carry. Also the custom of the said manor is that every of the said tenants shall reap one acre of wheat and bind it and set the sheaves on windrows [to dry off]. Also the custom is that every one of the said tenants shall mow one acre of barley and pook it [stack it]. Also the said tenants of Netherhampton claim certain duties, that is to say, to have for the earing and edging of wheat, as before is mentioned, amongst them all, 2s Item, the said tenants claim to have for the washing and shearing of the said sheep, 15d, and one pook of hay as they will choose it in Woodmiln Mead, or 6d Also for the mowing of Woodmiln Mead one fat sheep of the price of 16d Item, the said tenants claim of custom for reaping as above is specified, every tenant to have so much wheat as they may bind in a sheaf's bond. And in like manner every of them to have of barley as much as any of them may bind in a barley bond.'

Thus the works were not highly burdensome and did not go unrewarded. Elsewhere the services might include carting, as at nearby South Newton, where 'the tenants every year out of their goodwill shall carry for the lord housebote, firebote [building and fuel wood respectively] and timber to the lord's seat at Wilton upon reasonable request and summons, which carriage is called Gift Carriage, taking meat, bread and drink at the lord's costs'. In the Peak-Forest Country and wherever coal mines abounded, a service commonly met with was the carting of coals from the pit-head to the lord's house. At Woodstock, where the kings and queens had a residence, the tenants of one village had to carry hay to the deer in the park, those of another were bound to sweep and clean the manor house, and those of a third to clean the chimneys, privies and easements there. But such domestic chores were imposed only rarely.

Manors and Their Customs

The kingdom was divided into manors, lordships or halls, all of which amounted to much the same thing, and all the base service-tenants belonged to one or another of these. Sometimes the ground plan of a lordship coincided with that of the village or township with which it was associated, but often two or more neighbouring townships were all the tenants of a single manor, which then had a composite name perhaps, like Chilmark and Ridge, Bootle with Linacre, or Candelent and Capel with Newton in Trimley. Almost as frequently a single township would be divided amongst two or more manors, with suitably qualified names, such as Burbage Esturmy, Burbage Savage alias Seymours, and Burbage Darrells, or Shalbourne Westcourt and Shalbourne Eastcourt. Manors or lordships could be in either single or joint ownership, and of course it often happened that many of them were held by one great lord.

The heart of the manor lay in its courts or hallmoots. The franklins or frank or free tenants (as opposed to base ones) had their court baron, where the lord's steward acted as registrar and the franklins or barons judged among themselves. The others, the villeins, or base or customary tenants, had their customary court, where the steward stood in the same relation to the jury as did the judge in the king's courts. The jury judged the facts of the case and gave a verdict, while the steward looked up and expounded the custom or law of the manor and passed sentence. Even in the customary court, let it be noted, all trial was by jury, and the lord was no more above the custom of the manor than the king was above the common law of the land. The rule of law obtained in the one as in the other, that is, no man ruled any other, but all men were ruled by the law.

The word 'custom' is now used in the sense of a set form of
behaviour, such as drinking cocoa before retiring for the night
or shrinking the heads of one's enemies. But it formerly meant
something quite different. 'Custom' used to mean what we now
call 'law', and the common law or custom of the land was the
common sense or consensus of opinion of all the local laws or
customs.

Manorial customs were concerned chiefly with agriculture,
service-tenancies, real estate, and country life in general. They
were the local land laws that governed the relations between base
service-tenants and their lords and originated in the conveyances
made and rules laid down in the manor courts. In the first place
these tenants had been mostly illiterate and had of necessity conducted their land business by word of mouth before witnesses
in open court, just as they had bought and sold their goods
before witnesses in an open market-place. There was no other
way to record transactions. They conveyed their property in
their land holdings by word of mouth in open court by sur-
rendering their holdings back to the lord of the manor to the
use of a third party. The lord accepted the surrender and then
granted the land to the third party who had been named. The
court thus became a registry of such transactions. The customs
or laws by which these lands were held, occupied and conveyed
from one tenant to another were the customs of the manor.

The lands held of the lord of a manor and so conveyed in his
courts were called by the Anglo-Saxons 'folkland', by the
Normans, 'villein land', in later times, 'bondland' or land of base
tenure, and, finally, 'customary land'. All these names meant and
amounted to one and the same thing: the land was held at the
will (or by the wish) of the lord according to the custom of the
manor. This is how the customary tenants we constantly meet
with in Tudor and Stuart times acquired their name. Then, with
the spread of literacy, the customary and other manorial courts
took to having their transactions recorded in writing on parch-
ment rolls. Once this was done and literacy had percolated
further down the social scale, the customary tenant found it to
his advantage to buy from the steward of the manor a certified

copy of the entry in the rolls that related to his own holding; he then became a copyholder. And this is the origin and nature of the copyholders we are always reading about in olden times, and even until fairly recently, for some lingered on until 1921, when the legal category was finally abolished. In Tudor and Stuart England, the vast majority of manorial tenants were copyholders like this and probably held between them a half or two-thirds of all the land of the kingdom.

Common Lands and Common Fields

Roughly speaking, the base service-tenants and the copyholders were one and the same people. When the great estates had been broken up, half the land had been distributed among service-tenants whose successors were the copyholders of early modern England. But it was not only land that had been distributed. The flocks, herds and teams needed to cultivate and manure the land were necessarily apportioned in much the same way. As for the demesne lands, they were largely cultivated for the lords or their farmers by the self-same service tenants. All told, then, most of English agriculture had been run mainly by individual families in a small way of business. And it was this division amongst a multitude of petty family businesses that gave rise to common rights, common lands and common fields.

Where the service-tenancy system was applied to meadowland, it gave rise to common meadows. The meadows were divided and allotted among the tenants, either according to the swathes of grass as they came from the scythe, or else in long parcels or pieces of land, which had been staked out after measuring along the shorter and opposite sides of the meadow and were subsequently marked off from each other by merestones and other landmarks. Sometimes the meadow was parcelled out on a permanent basis, but often lots were cast again every year, usually by putting the men's names or brand-marks into a hat and drawing lots to decide the rota for distribution of what were then called lot meadows. But either way, the greater the number of tenants, the smaller the allotments.

Where the service-tenancy system was applied to rough

grazings, the land itself was neither divided nor allotted. Since the people knew no method of square measurement, great expanses of land could not be easily and fairly parcelled out among them. Where the grazing was so extensive that there was more than enough for everybody, as frequently happened in mountainous districts, no action needed to be taken. Elsewhere, not the land itself, but the right to put livestock into it was the object of division. Each tenant was given a quota or stint of animals that he was allowed to put onto the commons, according to the size of his arable holdings and so of his livestock requirements. Thus a standard holding might put in, say, thirty sheep, two or three cows and a couple of horses. Then, as the number of tenants rose and fell, the stints could be changed accordingly.

It still sometimes happened that plots in these common pastures were selected for temporary cultivation, and then the tillage in them would be distributed by casting lots, using the same scale of rates applied in stinting the commons for grazing. Where the plot was ploughed ridge-and-furrow, it was split lengthways of the ridges and each cultivator was allotted so many ridges dispersed in such-and-such a regular order throughout what thus became a temporary common field, sometimes called 'lot acres'.

Where the service-tenancy system was applied to permanent tillage fields, it similarly gave rise to permanent common fields. Here the area involved was usually much greater than in either common meadows or lot acres, and its division was so much the more difficult and complicated. It was made easier, however, by virtue of the fact that the field consisted of a number of blocks called furlongs, which were laid out as the lie of the land and the nature of the soils dictated, the object being to group together, as far as possible, similar kinds of land (*figure* 10, *plate* 12). Thus a field might contain a Sandy Furlong, a Clay Furlong, a Hill Furlong, and so on. Each furlong in each field would be divided lengthways of the ridges, simply by walking along and counting off so many ridges to each man in turn. Each parcel of ridges would then be bounded with merestones and usually by leaving a boundary balk of unploughed ground that also served

D

as a path between the parcels (*plate 11*). Naturally, if the field
had not been ploughed before, the parcels would have to be
measured off in the first instance by measuring along both ends
of the furlong with poles or yardsticks. But this would not need
to be done more than once, for when the land had been ploughed,
the furrows between the ridges would mark the bounds of the
parcels and a boundary balk could then be left to separate one

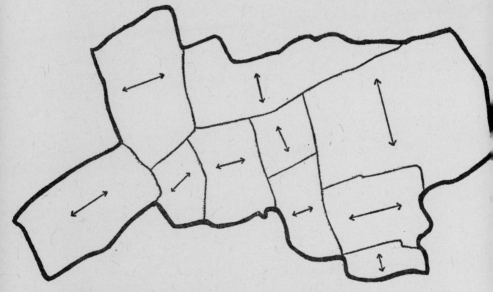

Fig. 10.   A great field divided into furlongs, redrawn from a map of 1635.
The field itself is enclosed, but the furlongs lie open to each other. The arrows
indicate the approximate direction of ploughing.

man's land from another's. In this way the furlong came to be
divided up into parcels of measured acres, or of multiples or
fractions of an acre, with each parcel containing as many ridges
as the ploughing required. As the number of tenants increased
and the holdings were further subdivided, these long parcels
could thus easily be split up smaller and smaller, and the smaller
the narrower. At the same time, by the same process, the various
parcels that went to make up any individual holding became
ever more scattered and dispersed amongst those belonging to

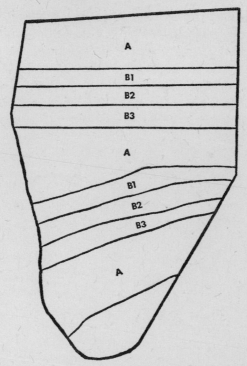

Fig. 11. Diagram to show how land became divided up and dispersed in common fields. The furlong and the parcels in it are shown in the 1635 map (see figure 10); but the division of the land between A and B and the subdivision of B's land between B1, B2 and B3 are imaginary.

others, so that the different holdings became almost inextricably intermingled (*figure 11*).

Common-field Regulations. The further division and subdivision proceeded, the greater became the mingle-mangle in the common fields, and so much greater the care needed to co-ordinate the operations of the various commoners. If they were to plough, sow, and harvest without getting in each other's way, they all had to plough, sow and harvest at much the same time and put their stock into the fallows and send their flocks from hill to field and back again at agreed times on agreed days. They had also to stint the numbers of sheep, cows and horses put into the stubble and fallow fields, lest one man's stock ate out another's. These considerations, and the obvious advantages which the division of labour involved, induced the tenantry to put all their cattle in common herds under common herdsmen and their sheep into common flocks and folds under common shepherds. The tenants assembled in their town meetings and agreed upon all the orders and rates needed for commoning, for regulating the common fields, and for running the common services. Their decisions were then normally announced in, and recorded and enforced by the manorial courts.

Common fields were often called 'town fields', especially towards the north and west of England. In one way this term was the more apt, for 'common' simply meant 'public' and the public body concerned was the township. Yet it was only the regulation of common fields that was the business of the town, for the parcels of land in the fields, like the allotments of meadow and the rights to common of pasture, were all strictly private property.

Although many fields that were not common were open and unenclosed, and some common fields, or parts of them, were enclosed with hedges and ditches, most of them had no permanent protection. In order to defend their crops against farm and other animals, the little common-field farmers set up round their corn fields a dead hedge or temporary fence, which could be taken down or thrown open after harvest. For the rest they relied on common herdsmen and shepherds, with their boys and dogs, to see that the sheep did not get into the meadows nor the cows into the corn.

Common-field agriculture was not necessarily inferior to that in undivided or severalty ground. As long as the demesne was cultivated by tenants' services, or in so far as it was, the skills employed there and in the common fields were almost identical. In each, the general plan of management, the field-courses, crop-rotations, implements, livestock and everything else were much the same. The tenants could hardly have shown more skill on the demesne than on their own holdings and frequently displayed less zeal on their lord's than on their own land.

Moreover, while it is true that the customary works on the demesne were closely supervised by the lord's officers, the town governments themselves performed much the same function in the common fields and prevented their husbandry falling below standard. They enforced appropriate field-courses and thereby prohibited harmful crop rotations. When the balance between corn and grass needed altering, it was the township that controlled the conversion entailed. From the fourteenth to the eighteenth century common-field cultivators in the Midland Plain and other areas suited to permanent grass tended to lay more and more of their tillage to greensward. When this had been done, the lands were called 'leylands' or 'leys' and the headlands 'headleys'. What with these, and the common balks or greenways and boundary balks or green furrows, about half of many of these common fields became permanent grass. This was a better balance and pushed corn yields on the remaining tillage up to as high as ten grains harvested for every one sown. Standards of cultivation were enforced in many other ways too. It was forbidden to sell straw, muck and compost off the farm or, at least, out of the township. Occupiers were under compulsion to extirpate thistles and other weeds. Pigs had to have their snouts ringed to stop them grubbing up commonable lands at pleasure, and cows their horns knobbed with pieces of wood to prevent them damaging persons and property. Mangy horses, distempered cattle and rotten sheep were debarred the commons. Animals dying of infectious diseases had to be buried deep and well out of the way. The township also saw to it that only 'good and sufficient' bulls, rams, and boars were allowed to run with the common herds and flocks. It ordered the extermination of pests and vermin, including crows, ravens, jackdaws, sparrows and moles; organized parties to destroy crows' nests, and rewarded those who brought in tallies of their kill. It employed shepherds, cowherds, molecatchers and other public servants, not forgetting the human scarecrows normally used at a time before dummies were resorted to. Finally, it provided genuinely collective goods like ponds, pumps (*plate 31*), trenching ploughs and hay for the common flocks, which could not be supplied to any without being available to all, and paid for them out of taxes rated on the townsfolk in strict proportion to the benefits enjoyed by them, which depended on the size of their farms.

Common fields of this kind were found in most countries, the only complete exceptions being the Vale of Taunton Deane, the Wealden Vales, the High Weald, and Romney Marsh, which consisted largely of land brought into cultivation only at a relatively late date. In some other countries where it was not worth while having much permanent tillage, in the Cheshire Cheese Country and the Lancashire Plain for example, the common fields never became very large. The Northdown, Saltings and Sandlings Countries, the Woodland, High Suffolk and East Norfolk all had their common fields in earlier times, but developed them less, and in a less complicated form than elsewhere, and started to abandon them rather sooner. By about 1500 the common fields in these countries had mostly been superseded, leaving only remnants and superficial traces. Why this happened is to be explained by the converse of our same former argument. Parcelling out land and livestock in successively smaller portions created common fields. But where land and stock were divided and subdivided to a lesser extent or not at all, common fields either did not emerge, or did so only in a rudimentary form that when the time came could all the more easily be dissolved. Why then, in these places, was the tillage much less divided up? The answer seems to be that a father would only share his land and stock out amongst all his sons if he could not provide for the younger ones in any other and better way. Nor, if there were any reasonable alternative, would any of them have wished to have taken over a tiny and almost unworkable holding. The rising generation had to be provided for by subdividing the holding only where land was virtually the only form of wealth. This was the situation where agriculture was relatively unprofitable and where decent openings in other walks of life were lacking. Common fields, therefore, developed to their greatest extent where these conditions existed, which meant, above all, in the landlocked midland region. By contrast, in the eastern countries of England more wealth could be accumulated from agriculture, and capital was available to start alternative businesses in manufacturing and transporting. It was no mere chance or coincidence that made the rich agricultural east and south of England the chief seat of both industry and commerce, as well as the cradle of the greatest and capital city. In these parts, either the land was not cut up into small holdings, or, if it had been, was soon consolidated again by knocking many small farms together into fewer and larger ones. This entailed getting rid of any common fields that existed, for big farmers had no conceivable use for them. Of course, it was in this way and for these reasons that all the common fields were eventually enclosed in all parts of the kingdom: as the land became formed into large farms in a few hands, common fields were nothing but a nuisance. But for the time being, until agriculture, industry and trade made the necessary advances, people in landlocked parts like the Midland Plain had little alternative but to eke out a precarious existence on the land, which had consequently to be parcelled out in holdings so small as to be manageable only in common fields.

The Different Kinds of Country People

One way and another, what with the land being in many places broken up into little tillage farms in common fields, and in parts of the south-east lying in capital or large farms, with the special character of life in and around the fens and forests, and the conversion of much of certain areas to grazing fat stock and dairy cows, there had developed, by the sixteenth century, several distinctive and often sharply contrasting types of country-folk. 'Husbandmen', it was said, 'are much the same in all districts: plain, frugal, painstaking, close and unintelligible.' But while these characteristics were to some extent common to all, remarkable differences inevitably developed between the service-tenants, many of them copyholders, who earned their livings in the common fields; the family farmers who had turned their land over to dairying; the capital farmers, some of whom worked alongside their men; and the landowners who ran their own home farms.

Common-field Farmers. The saying, that 'poverty and ignorance are the ordinary inhabitants of small farms', applies with peculiar force to the little common-field farmer. He is generally acknowledged to be active and industrious, but what this means in practice is that he 'will toil all his days, himself and his family, for nothing, in and upon his common arable field land, up early and down late, drudge and moil and wear out himself and his family'. As another observer puts it, 'The labour of these men is great and circular or endless, insomuch that their bodies are almost in constant weariness and their minds in constant care or trouble'. Such men did all the work on the farm, for hands were hired only if the husband were dead or able-bodied sons were lacking, and even then none but inferior workmen could be attracted, for the wages were low and the work unspecialized. All that happened was that someone else took over the same old treadmill. It was said of such farmers, 'Their servants are so heavy with early rising and hard working that they cannot attend to what they hear'.

Every spring the petty common-field farmer had the utmost difficulty in bridging the gap between his fast-disappearing stock of straw and hay and his sparse and slow-sprouting grass. It was proverbial among these men that 'Lide pills the hide', meaning that March pinches the poor man's beast. And if and when the harvest failed, as occasionally it was bound to do, the old saw sprang readily to mind, that 'Hunger sets his first foot into the horse-manger', which is to say, the farmer and his family were themselves fain to eat what they normally gave their horses. The farmer first starved his beasts, and then his land, and then himself. As Richard Baxter tells us in 1691, the poor husbandman and his family,

'are glad of a piece of hanged bacon once a week, and some few that can kill a bull eat now and then a bit of hanged beef enough to tire the stomach of an ostrich. He is a rich man that can afford to eat a joint of fresh meat (beef, mutton or veal) once a month or fortnight. If their sow pig or their hens breed chickens, they cannot afford to eat them, but must sell them to make their rent.

They cannot afford to eat the eggs that their hens lay nor the apples or pears that grow on their trees (save some that are not vendible) but must make money of all. All the best of their butter and cheese they must sell and feed themselves and children and servants with skimmed cheese and skimmed milk and whey curds.'

In the words of John Earle's thumbnail sketch in 1628, such

'a plain country fellow is one that manures his ground well, but lets himself lie fallow and untilled. He has reason enough to do his business and not enough to be idle and melancholy. He seems to have the judgement of Nebuchadnezzar, for his conversation is among beasts. . . . His hand guides the plough and the plough his thoughts, and his ditch and landmark is the very mound of his meditations. He expostulates with his oxen very understandingly, and speaks Gee and Ree better than English. His mind is not much distracted with objects, but if a good fat cow come in his way, he stands dumb and astonished, and though his haste be never so great, will fix here half an hour's contemplation. His habitation is some poor thatched roof (distinguished from his barn by the loopholes that let out smoke), which the rain had long since washed through, but for the double ceiling of bacon on the inside, which has hung there from his grandsire's time and is yet to make rashers for posterity. His dinner is his other work, for he sweats at it as much as at his labour. He is a terrible fastener on a piece of beef and you may hope to stave the guard off sooner. His religion is part of his copyhold, which he takes from his landlord and refers it wholly to his discretion. Yet if he give him leave, he is a good Christian to his power, that is, comes to church in his best clothes and sits there with his neighbours, where he is capable only of two prayers, for rain and fair weather.'

The Dairy-grazers. Where the family farmers had gone over to dairy-grazing, as in the Cheese Country and the Vale of Berkeley, things were quite different. This was partly because in the process of going over to grass and setting up dairy farms, which were largely in owner-occupation, the old manors had been dismembered and broken up and their courts discontinued. As a result, John Aubrey noticed in North Wiltshire, 'the mean people live lawless, nobody to govern them, they care for nobody, having no dependence on anybody'. But there was more to it than that, and the same observer gives us his further thoughts on these people in these terms:

'Wood sorrel and such acid herbs naturally produced in clay lands make an acidness in their complexions, fire their spirits, make them lazy and contemplative and venereous. Hence comes their great search into religion—most of them are fanatics. The natives here are fair and plump. In the hill country the natives are dry, more active and industrious, no good singers. In the north part they sing very well, and the milkmaid will sing so shrill and clear. . . . The indigenae or aborigines speak drawling. . . . Hereabout is but little tillage or hard labour. They only milk cows and make cheese. They feed chiefly on milk meats, which cool their brains too much and hurts their inventions. These circumstances make them melancholy, contemplative and malicious, by consequence thereof come more lawsuits out of North Wiltshire, at least double the number to the southern parts. . . . It is a sour, woodsere country, and inclines people to contemplation, so that, and the Bible, and ease, for it is all now upon dairy-grazing and clothing, sit there with a-running and reforming.'

Perhaps we need not follow all Aubrey's reasoning in order to be convinced he was right about the dairy-graziers' relatively easy life and high degree of independence from landlords and town governments making them a race apart from the common-field farmers. They were as different as chalk and cheese.

The Fenmen. Aubrey also drew a distinction between the husband-men on the downs and the wolds and the fen-dwellers. The former he found not only more active and industrious but also, 'of a very cheerful humour, affable and courteous in their deport-ment, not sparing or profuse in their entertainments, but of a generous temper suitable to the sweet and healthful air they do dwell in, whereas the inhabitants of boggy, fenny countries are of a more surly, jealous and inhospitable humour'.

The truth of this is well illustrated in the Fen Country itself. As the fens were remote, unhealthy and dangerous, the only people who lived in them were stockmen, shepherds, cottagers, and, above all, squatters. These 'breedlings' and 'slodgers', Camden tells us, dwelt in cabins on islets amidst the watery wastes. They were 'rude, uncivil, and envious to all others, whom they call "upland men"; who, stalking on high upon stilts, apply their minds to grazing, fishing and fowling'.

The marshes near the east and south coasts were made somewhat less unpleasant and unhealthy by better drainage and sea-breezes, but they could still give a painful ague to strangers who went fowling in them. Defoe relates with some relish the perhaps slightly exaggerated information that many farmers in the Saltings Country had run through fifteen or more wives, the record seemingly being held by a man living with his twenty-fifth wife, whose 35-year-old son had still only attained to his fourteenth. This was because hardened natives of the marshlands chose upland brides who soon sickened in the fogs and damps below the cliff. Defoe also notes that the poor people who lived all their lives in the marshes themselves seldom reached any great age. A stranger going into these marshes even now may find his breathing more laboured, his spirits depressed and his limbs heavy, and the 'dags' or heavy morning mists have grown no more pleasant with the years. Improved drainage did much to better the lot of the fen-dwellers in the Fen Country in the seventeenth century, but it was said they were much more pestered with gnats than before, and even in the nineteenth century many people there could only dull the edge of their agues by taking opium. The 'slodgers' in earlier times were understandably an impoverished, disgruntled and barely civilized breed of men.

The Forest-dwellers. A different race again lived in and around the forests, particularly the more thickly wooded ones. Wooded or not, the forests were ex-parochial land used by the monarchs as their hunting grounds and therefore subject to special forest laws aimed at the preservation of the chase. This alone marked all forest-dwellers out from other people. But it was the woods that gave many of them their own walk of life. These men were not really agriculturalists. They engaged in a little desultory agriculture, but combined this with relics of the hunting and collecting economies of a bygone age. They bore far less resemblance to most English farmers than to the pioneers or first settlers in the woodland parts of North America and are best regarded as being in the one and same class as the latter 'half barbarous race'. The English forest-settlers had mostly run up their cabins in a single day in order to claim dubious squatters' rights by having smoke coming from the roof by nightfall. They normally grew a little corn, but were more concerned with their cattle and sheep, which they put to graze in the lawns and grassy glades between the woods and copses. They bred swine and fed and fattened them on acorns and beechmast. They gathered nuts, berries and wild honey for food and sticks and underwood for fuel. And they were all poachers, delighting especially in hunting the royal deer with crossbows, for the benefit of their own pots and to sell to the neighbouring butchers and purveyors of venison. They systematically broke every restriction placed upon them and abused every right they laid title to. Where they were allowed sticks on the ground, they tore boughs from the trees. If they were permitted to take dead trees, they peeled off the bark to kill good ones. When they were suffered to feed their hogs on the masts, 'ungovernable multitudes' from miles around invaded the woods, 'shaking and dashing the trees' to get mast to sell as an ordinary article of commerce. No conker season ever saw the like. Taking advantage of permission to shelter their sheep in safe arbours in time of storm, they put whole flocks into the woods day in and day out, so that the new shoots were eaten off and killed.

It is hardly surprising that observers noted in common-field townships in and near the forests 'a new brood of upstart intruders, as inmates and inhabitants of unlawful cottages . . .

loiterers who will not usually be got to work unless they have such excessive wages as they themselves desire'. As they are 'permitted to live in idleness upon their stock of cattle', they become 'so many naughty and idle persons' who 'will bend themselves to no kind of labour'. John Norden soon found in Wales that 'Cottagers are noisome neighbours unto the forests, for they and their goats confound the underwoods as fast as they grow'. They are 'given to little or no kind of labour, living very hardly with oaten bread, sour whey and goats' milk, dwelling far from any church or chapel, and are as ignorant of God or of any civil course of life as the very savages among the infidels'. The lawlessness and barbarity of the forest-dwellers was indeed a byword among contemporaries and Norden was only voicing the general opinion when he said the forests themselves were 'so ugly a monster as of necessity will breed more and more idleness, beggary and atheism, and consequently disobedience to God and the King'. Into these places, he says, 'infinite poor, yet most idle inhabitants have thrust themselves, living covertly without law or religion, rude and refractory by nature, amongst whom are nourished and bred infinite idle fry, that coming ripe grow vagabonds and infect the commonwealth with the most dangerous leprosies'.

The Borderers. Another race apart were the peasants who lived on the borders of England and Scotland. These were a servile lot of people, whose lords could command them in all things as they wished and extract from them at pleasure whatever money they happened to have. The Earl of Cumberland was not alone in having 'a brutish sort of tenants, that if my lord take their wives, they dare not oppose him'. A little primitive agriculture and some cattle-breeding went hand in hand with the no less important occupation of stealing, in which the chief specialization was in cattle-rustling. This was a seasonal employment, being conducted in winter, when cattle-breeding demanded little attention. In summer, which was the close season for thieving, the men attended their herds and lands. Over and above these mere peasant industries, there were bands of moss-troopers or professional criminals on both sides of the border. These stole all the year round in the normal course of business, but had a field-day of cattle-rustling (and worse crimes) when the part-time thieves or their womenfolk and families were summering with 'their' cattle in the glens amidst the hills and mountains.

The Graziers. Travelling southwards now to the Midland Plain and the vale lands of southern and western England, we ascend to the upper part of the social scale and meet the graziers who worked the great expanses of land laid down from permanent tillage to permanent grass. Such graziers operated on very large acreages and were necessarily rather few in number. They were also well-to-do and lived like gentlemen without soiling their hands with manual labour. Indeed, they were frequently also landowners on some scale and members of county or noble families. Success in the grazier's walk of life turned on the possession of ample working capital to allow the uninhibited purchase and sale of livestock, and on the acumen needed in judging lean and fat stock and watching all the ups and downs of the markets.

Such graziers and their landlords were the subject of much prejudiced and jaundiced comment, possibly the best informed of which came from the pen of Sir Thomas More in his *Utopia*:

'Noblemen and gentlemen, yes, and certain abbots, holy men God wot . . . enclose all in pastures. They throw down houses, they pluck down towns, and leave nothing standing but only the church, to make of it a sheephouse. . . . One covetous and insatiable cormorant and very plague of his native country may compass about and enclose many thousands of acres of ground together within one pale or hedge. . . . These rich men bring up not the younger ones of great cattle as they do lambs, but first they buy them abroad very cheap, and afterwards, when they be fatted in their pastures, they sell them again exceeding dear.'

In the mid-seventeenth century, when permanent grass had almost gone by the board, Walter Blith's attack on the grazier was along somewhat different lines. His great crime now is that he will not grow any corn. He

'will not plough any old pasture land at all, upon any terms, or for any time. . . . He will not have it ploughed come what will. "What", saith he, "destroy my old pasture, my sheepwalks, and beggar my land!" All the world will not persuade him to do that. You may as soon persuade him not to eat good wholesome food, because some men overcharged their stomachs by excess herein. Because here and there an indiscreet man did wrong his land by excessive ploughing, he will not use it at all. . . . "No", saith he, "I can raise a constant profit by my wool and lamb, my fat beef and mutton, at an easy quiet way unto myself and family, without much vexing and turmoiling." . . . He takes more content in a shepherd and his dog and in his own will and ease than in greater advantage. . . . He is seated in the way of feeding and grazing, with a constant stock of breeding, and let his land be fit for one or fit for another use, he matters it not. He hath received a prejudice against ploughing. . . . Let it be dry or moist, sound or rotten, rushy or mossy, fenny or run over with flag-grass or anthills, moss or wild thyme, let it keep more or less, he'll not alter.'

This is clearly the picture of a stick-in-the-mud who no longer bothers to try and maximize his profits. It is all the easier for us to believe because we have seen the same men in modern dress. During the last war, when corn-growing was both profitable and patriotic, a few graziers obstinately refused to plough up their old pastures, and some even resisted the efforts of the war agricultural executive committees to come and do it for them. Some fields had to be invaded by columns of tractors for all the world like tanks entering enemy territory. And I myself have heard a grazier declare a field of grass and weeds unploughable, even though the very thistles grew in the ridges and furrows set up by former ploughmen. Small wonder that graziers excited hostility from those who saw their donkey-pastures. They were all dog-and-stick men and appeared to the farmer to do little more than lean on a gate and watch the weeds grow.

The Capital Farmers. It was a far cry from these graziers to the capital farmers who, by the early sixteenth century, had emerged in parts of south-eastern England. These, we are told, 'be [for the most part] farmers unto gentlemen, which . . . with keeping servants not idle as the gentleman doth, but such as get both their own living and part of their master's . . . do come to such wealth that they are able and daily to buy the lands of unthrifty gentlemen'. To be a little more exact, these capital farmers may be divided into two types. First, there was the working farmer, who not only employed farm labourers and managed and oversaw the farm as a whole, but also acted as his own foreman and went out to the fields with his men. Secondly, there was the rather rarer gentleman farmer who kept his hands clean and left even the supervision of work to a foreman, bailiff or chief servant. Where the working farmer said to his men, 'Let's go to the field', the gentleman said, 'Go to the field'. So ingrained was this distinction that the language, in Wessex at least, used to have distinct words for the purpose. 'In the familiar difference of the usual words "gay and go" ', writes John Smyth of Nibley, 'consisteth half the thrift of my husbandries. *Gay* is let us go, when myself goes as one of the company; but *go* is the sending of others when myself stays behind.'

Thomas Overbury in 1615 gives us an excellent sketch of a typical working farmer:

'Though he be master, he says not to his servants, "Go to field", but "Let us go"; and with his own eye doth fatten his flocks and set forward all manner of husbandry. He is taught by nature to be contented with a little; his own fold yields him both food and raiment. He is pleased with any nourishment God sends, whilst curious gluttony ransacks, as it were, Noah's Ark for food, only to feed the riot of one meal. He is never known to go to law, understanding to be law-bound among men is like to be hidebound among his beasts: they thrive not under it; and that such men sleep as unquietly as if their pillows were stuffed with lawyers' penknives. When he builds, no poor tenant's cottage hinders his prospect: they are indeed his alms-

houses, though there be painted on them no such superscription.
. . . He is not so inquisitive after news derived from the privy
closet, when the finding of an eyrie of hawks in his own ground
or the foaling of a colt come of a good strain are tidings more
pleasant, more profitable.'

Although he was fashioned out of the same stuff, the gentleman farmer was a cut above this. John Norden was much struck
by 'another sort of husbandman . . . and that not a few, who
wade in the weeds of gentlemen. These only oversee their
husbandry and give direction unto their servants, seldom or not
at all setting their hand unto the plough.' To John Stephens, in
1615, the gentleman farmer,

'is a concealed commodity. His worth or value is not known till
he be half rotten, and then he is worth nothing. He hath religion
enough to say, "God bless His Majesty, God send peace and
fair weather," so that one may glean harvest out of him to be
the time of his happiness. But the tithe-sheaf goes against his
conscience, for he had rather spend the value upon his reapers
and ploughmen than bestow anything to the maintenance of a
parson. He is sufficiently book-read, nay, a profound doctor,
if he can search into the diseases of cattle; and to foretell rain by
tokens makes him a miraculous astronomer. To speak good
English is more than he much regards; and for him not to
contemn all arts and languages were to contemn his own educa-
tion. The pride of his housekeeping is a mess of cream, a pig,
or a green goose; and if his servants can uncontrolled find the
highway to the cupboard, it wins the name of a bountiful yeoman. Doubtless he would murmur against the tribune's law, by
which none might occupy more than five hundred acres, for he
murmurs against himself because he cannot purchase more. . . .
To peruse the statutes and prefer them before the Bible makes
him purchase the credit of a shrewd fellow, and then he can
bring all his adversaries to composition; and if at length he can
discover himself in large legacies beyond expectation, he hath
his desire. Meantime, he makes the prevention of dearth his title
to be thought a good commonwealth's man. And therefore he

E

preserves a chandler's treasure of bacon, links and puddings in the chimney corner. He is quickly and contentedly put into the fashion, if his clothes be made against Whitsuntide or Christmas Day, and then outwardly he contemns appearance. He cannot therefore choose but hate a Spaniard likewise and he thinks that hatred alone makes him a loyal subject, for benevolences and subsidies be more unseasonable to him than his quarter's rent. Briefly, being a good housekeeper, he is an honest man; and so he thinks of rising no higher but rising early in the morning; and, being up, he hath no end of motion, but wanders in his woods and pastures so continually that when he sleeps or sits he wanders also.'

Lastly, we should note that many small landowners and squires kept their demesne lands in their own hands and cultivated them themselves, thus being landlords and capital farmers rolled into one. They were thus at the top of the farming ladder. Such a cultivating squire would rank among the middling gentry and could aspire to sitting on the bench. Overbury describes such a squire as:

'a thing out of whose corruption the generation of a justice of peace is produced. He speaks statutes and husbandry well enough to make his neighbours think him a wise man. He is well skilled in arithmetic and rates, and hath eloquence enough to save his twopence. His conversation amongst his tenants is desperate, but amongst his equals full of doubt. His travel is seldom farther than the next market town, and his inquisition is about the price of corn. . . . Nothing under a subpoena can draw him to London, and when he is there, he sticks fast upon every object, casts his eye away upon gazing, and becomes the prey of every cutpurse. When he comes home, those wonders serve him for his holiday talk. . . . By this time he hath learned to kiss his hand and make a leg both together, and the names of the lords and councillors. He hath thus much toward entertainment and courtesy, but of the last he makes more use, for by the recital of "My lord" he conjures his poor countrymen. But this is not his element. He must home again, being like a dor that ends his flight in a dunghill.'

Chapter Three

THE FARMING COUNTRIES

What Countries Were

England in 1560 was a world in itself, with its own Alps, its own Holland, and almost every other variety of country. Not all the people in this kingdom spoke English. Celtic tongues were still heard in Cornwall and in the mountains of Wales. Nor did England include all the English-speakers, for many of these were to be found in the kingdoms of Scotland and Ireland. But what was happening was that the increasing division of labour, by which individuals in various places came to specialize in producing particular goods and services with the object of exchanging them by way of trade, was systematically knitting all these peoples together to form one English or British nation.

For political and administrative purposes the English kingdom had long been divided into counties, and if we were dealing with such matters, these counties and their intricate boundaries would loom large in our minds. But, of course, these counties never had anything to do with agriculture or rural life. Farming was not carried on according to counties, so we can disregard them with a clear conscience. Instead, the geographical region or unit that will concern us here is the country, and we shall have to make the acquaintance of the two score or so countries into which England was divided, and which have been mapped out in the frontispiece to this book.

By these countries English people meant much what the French mean now when they speak of *pays*. To the urbanized Englishmen of the present day, this no doubt seems a strange thing, for when we say 'country' we mean to distinguish either our nation and state from others, or else to indicate the un-developed as opposed to the built-up parts. This being so, our first and natural reaction on meeting the word in its old sense,

67

will probably be to say, 'Of course, when these people said "country" they meant "county" ', and so to make an end of it. But to do this would really be to deny our own ancestors the credit of being able to make out the spoken word and attach meaning to it. And even though we flatter ourselves we are more intelligent than they were, we should in all honesty admit that they knew their own world in a way we shall never be able to. As a matter of fact, 'country' is only one of a number of words whose meaning has since been changed—or should we not say distorted? The word 'town', to take an interesting example, used to mean what we are now reduced to calling an 'inhabited point' and included hamlets, villages, towns and cities in our sense. This meant in practice that the words 'town' and 'township' were most often used, as they still are in North America, to designate what we should regard as 'country places'.

Your old farmer or cottager—'countryman' if you will— thought of himself as belonging to his own town and township, and in a wider world, to his own country. Take for instance the early seventeenth-century townsfolk of Woodmancote. They come together at a town meeting and decide their field-course (or system of cultivation) is 'unhusbandly', or as we should say, uneconomic, and that they ought to change it and follow the 'usage and custom of the Vale of Evesham, within the precinct of which they lie'. What most distinguished this Vale of Evesham country from the others round about was that the ploughlands were divided into four shifts or fields of a field-course that completed its cycle in just four years; and it was exactly this four-field course that Woodmancote township had made up its mind to use in future. These good people clearly did not regard the Vale of Evesham, in the sense they were using, as a natural region, for they knew very well that Woodmancote was not in what is now named the Vale of Evesham or of Red Horse. It was well inside the natural region that our geographer friends call the Vale of Gloucester or of Tewkesbury. But these were practical men coming to a decision about their own businesses and the thought of natural regions no more entered their heads than did the notion of counties. What they meant by the Vale of Evesham was the country where the four-field course, and all that went with it, was generally practised. In this sense, as it happened, the Vale of Evesham included also most of the natural region called the Vale of Gloucester. Here, in this farming country called the Vale of Evesham, most townships found the four-field course economic, and the people of Woodmancote, which was still stuck with a three-field one, thought it high time they caught up with their fellow countrymen.

How the Countries Originated

How the various countries came into existence and were gradually perfected can easily be understood. Alexander Pope once went into raptures over the joys of being a self-sufficient peasant or subsistence farmer:

> Happy the man whose wish and care
> A few paternal acres bound,
> Content to breathe his native air,
> In his own ground.
> Whose herds with milk, whose fields with bread,
> Whose flocks supply him with attire,
> Whose trees in summer yield him shade,
> In winter fire.

Such a life would no doubt appear very attractive to someone who only liked eating bread and milk and preferred wearing home-made clothes fashioned out of home-made cloth from home-made yarn by a person who was equally skilled at milking cows and ploughing fields. But it should not be overlooked that these lines come from an *Ode on Solitude* and are applicable to a hermit. Most people, however, shun the solitary life in favour of the interchange of goods and services in society. Needless to say, for it is only human nature, each husbandman looked out for himself and his family to the best of his ability, and soon found out he could best husband and economize his and their efforts and resources, and make the most of these, by sticking to what he was best at and leaving other things for other people to do. In this way, all could live and let live. By specializing and dividing their labours, and then providing specialist services for each other—in a manner of speaking, by taking in one another's washing—everyone stood a chance of making the most of himself and of living in the best possible way, for the obvious reason that practice makes perfect and specialists get the most practice. A do-it-yourself society, therefore, where every man is a jack-of-all-trades, will always be poorer than the one in which the cobbler sticks to his last and leaves other men to their own trades.

In the rural life of old England, what each man could best turn his hand to depended largely on the environment into which he was born. It depended on whether the climate were wet or dry, the soil light or heavy, the roads good or bad, the market places near or far. Such things, however, hardly differed as between neighbour and neighbour or even between town and town. All variations of soil, climate and terrain tended to be focused and localized in distinct geographical regions. A comparative advantage in corn-growing was shared by most of the husbandmen of eastern England, and in grass-growing by most of those in the west. In these and a thousand and one other ways, the opportunities for specialization and the division of labour were concentrated and grouped in particular places. These opportunities for specialized husbandries were, of course, as old as the hills. The Idovers of Dauntsey, later so renowned amongst the butchers of Smithfield market as excellent fatting grounds for stock, were doubtless already just as good when the Saxons first came to live by that winding stream the Welsh called *wy dover*. The Wick that Hengist could have seen from Hengistbury Head would have made as good a dairy farm then as it did later. Possibilities for specialization were always there and had only to be taken advantage of, but their nature differed from place to place, and they had to be seized country by country.

The character of a country was formed largely through its livestock. What these originally were and later became depended on the way they were managed and mostly on the way they were fed. This is what farmers meant when they said, 'All breed is put in at the mouth'. If the Suffolk Duns gave a high, and the

Devons a low proportion of butter fat, this was, as the East Anglian husbandmen put it, because 'Good pasture made the best cattle'. If the Old Gloucester cows gave milk that was good in the Vale of Berkeley for cheese and in the Butter Country for butter, this was due to differences in soil and herbage. Grasslands in various places contain dissimilar grasses, but the self-same variety of grass grown in two different situations will taste differently and make somewhat different milk even when going through one and the same cow. Thus most of the land in the Cheese Country was sour and suitable for cheese, but in a few places there, if the farmers' wives tried to make cheese they could not stop it heaving, though they could make good enough butter. It is for such-like reasons that making a particular type of cheese is not simply a matter of following a certain recipe. Again, with cattle and sheep intended to be fattened for the butcher, it was often a positive advantage for them to have been bred and reared on poor grasslands. An ox that has survived the sparse feed of the moors of the North Country, or a sheep brought up on the mountain slopes of Wales, can hardly fail to do well and put on weight when put into a rich lowland pasture. Moreover, where the grasses grew in chalky or limy soil, as they did on many downs and hills, the animals that fed on them tended to grow big bones, and since the quantity of lean meat depended in the first instance on the size and weight of the bones the muscles had to move, this was just what the grazier and the butcher wanted. What was bred in the bone came out in the flesh.

Upbringing was also important in forming an animal's character. English farmers mostly raised their livestock in the open air, a practice that Frenchmen in a later age viewed with astonished admiration, and christened '*l'éducation sauvage*'. But in other respects methods of upbringing differed widely. The dairyman's great concern was obviously to wean his calves as soon as possible, so as to get the milk, but the specialist stock breeder wanted his calves to have the best possible start in life and allowed the cow to suckle them as long as she wanted. Moreover, in dairy herds the cows were put to the pail and took kindly to being milked, whereas in breeding ones they were unused and distinctly averse to it. It would not have been worth the effort and time to capture such a breeding cow and tie it down for forcible milking (which, of course, is why American cowboys had to drink black coffee amidst a sea of cows). Similarly with sheep, the lambs born to folded flocks became used to hurdles and folds from the tenderest age and took so instinctively to folding routines in later life that they usually found their own way from the downs to the particular acre in the arable field that the shepherd wanted to pen them on next. Mountain sheep, however, which from the start were given licence to roam almost at will and leap from rock to rock, could not be confined in an ordinary field, let alone a fold. Nothing short of a moat would keep them in.

Then, again, different kinds of land suited quite different animals. Sheep liked dry land, and chronically wet fields would soon kill off some kinds. Other breeds, however, were inured to the wet, and all sheep were safe where the fields were brackish. Soft, spongy soils were suitable for foals of the heavy breeds, for these needed big hooves to bear their eventual weights. On the other hand, fens and marshes could not bear very weighty animals, so that the heavy horses bred in them were best reared elsewhere. In these and a thousand and one other ways, the different kinds and breeds of livestock all found their various ways to the places and countries that suited them best. Farmers largely chose the seeds they wanted to sow, but their livestock were to a far greater extent aborigines of the countries they lived in, and it was the farm animals that lent a country much of its distinctive character.

But technical considerations were far from being the only ones in setting up the divisions of labour. It obviously paid some farmers to specialise in certain branches of agriculture for no better reason than that farmers elsewhere found it paid to neglect them. There are large parts of East Anglia and thereabouts, for example, where the land and climate combine to make agricultural conditions superior to those anywhere else in the world. Technically speaking, the farms here were best for all purposes and equally well suited to corn-growing, dairying, stockbreeding, or feeding fat stock. But other places could undertake stockraising, even though they could not possibly specialise in corn-growing. The East Anglians had an advantage in all these things, but, thanks to a climate that gave them the maximum number of good harvests, many of them found their greatest comparative advantage, their greatest edge over others, in corn-growing. This led them to neglect stockraising, and this in turn opened the doors of opportunity to hill-farmers, who now found it more economic, and more husbandly, to concentrate on raising stock rather than on growing corn. But once most East Anglians had become specialist corn-growers, a want of dairy produce made itself felt there, especially in cream, cream cheese and butter, for these could not very well be transported from the west of England. And this in turn meant that some East Anglians found it to their greatest economic advantage to take up dairying.

Thus each farmer strove to specialize in the line in which he had the greatest possible advantage over his competitors elsewhere. Then, having once become a specialist himself, he was dependent on the specialist services of others in their own lines. Thus all the specialists became interdependent: they all bought from each other. In this way, every line was produced in the most economical way in the place where it was most economical to produce it, so that the sum total of private advantages became equal to the greatest possible public benefit. In looking after himself each husbandman was serving others to the best of his ability. In this way, too, man found natural regions, but himself made the farming countries.

So far we have talked mostly in terms only of the main specialized branches of farming like corn-growing, dairying, and stockraising. When we get down to brass tacks, however, we soon find that each of these is an over-generalization. In a general or aggregate sense, of course, farmers grown corn, but corn itself is a generic term. Even in North America, where it signifies Indian corn, it is no less generic, for there are many varieties of maize. In England, the word 'corn' includes wheat, barley, rye, oats and so on; one of these in turn is a generic term for many different varieties of wheats, and so for the others. When it comes right down to it, what we are faced with is not specialization in corn-growing, or even in wheat-growing, but in growing some particular kind and quality of wheat. Similarly, it is true to say in a certain general sense that some farmers specialized in dairying; but if we go to any particular dairy farm or any one dairying country, we find that what was specialized in was usually butter or cheese, and if cheese, then some particular kind and quality of cheese, each made in a different way from differing kinds of grass, or, perhaps, from hay or something else. In the same general sense, some countries specialised in stock-raising; but in reality, this might be either stockbreeding or stockrearing or both, and then either sheep or cattle or horses, and if, say, sheep, then of one or another breed of sheep. There were as many permutations in this as there are in the football pools. No wonder, then, that the geographical division of labour had, by 1560, produced as many as forty-two distinct countries, not to mention the nondescript Bristol quarter (*see map at the front of the book*).

These countries were all of them in some way unlike all the others, and the most unlike were often situated at opposite ends of England. Sometimes, however, countries relatively close to each other in their nature and practices were at opposite ends of the compass. Likewise it often happened that utterly unlike countries were close neighbours to each other. The Chalk and Cheese Countries, which were as different as chalk and cheese, could not have laid closer to each other, and the Chiltern and Vale husbandries, hardly less unlike, were also carried on side by side.

The Countries and Their Societies

As well as geographical divisions of labour, social ones developed; but these social divisions of labour grew up country by country and fell into the same geographical framework. The long and short of it is, that it was corn-growing that demanded most of the labour involved in agriculture. It was ploughing, harrowing, sowing, tending, weeding, harvesting, and threshing that made the work. At the other extreme, livestock-breeding in the hill-farming countries demanded little more than a man and a dog. Somewhere between these two extremes lay dairy-grazing or dairy-farming pure and simple, which demanded little field-work, but where each cow needed a good deal of attention and tied the dairyman or milkmaid to the farm, day in and day out. The care of livestock was a very demanding occupation. The owner had to be prepared to stay up all night with a cow in labour or go in search of a lost lamb. 'A man may love well his cow though he kiss her not', but he is less likely to love another's. It was the sort of attention to be expected of an owner rather than of a servant. It is 'the master's eye doth feed the horse'. For these reasons stockbreeding and grass-dairying favoured family farmers who did their own work with their own hands or those of their families and neither gave nor took employment. In such a business the man who extends his operations beyond the abilities of his family only bites off more than he can chew, and loses by it.

In corn-growing, on the contrary, economies of scale could be made. However small an arable farm, it required its own plough-team, which was dear to buy, expensive to maintain, and only economic if kept fully employed. It was wasteful to keep horses eating their heads off. But the same team that could cultivate five acres and then be left kicking its heels could cope with fifty acres and be kept busy and earning money all the time. When five hundred acres were split into a five-acre holdings, a hundred teams would be needed, and when into fifty-acre ones, ten teams. But when it was all one great, capital farm, with all the horses always fully employed, still fewer would be required. Provided that the size of the farm was nicely calculated to keep all the horses busy, the larger the farm, the fewer horses needed for each acre of corn; and the fewer the horses, the fewer the servants or hired hands to work along with them. This meant, the larger the farm and the more the acres in corn, within reason, the less the cost of each bushel grown and harvested. In the great cereal-growing countries, then, such economies of scale led inevitably to more and more of the land being concentrated into capital farms in the hands of gentlemen or working farmers who employed people to work for them for wages. As the farms were big and expensive, they rose out of the range of most people's pockets, and this meant in turn that there were always plenty of folk only too pleased to go out to work, and all the more willingly since a tiny farm gave less income than could reasonably be expected from a good employer. Thus a social division of labour grew up in which both farmers and farm workers found their greatest comparative advantage in being specialists in one or the other capacity.

In these ways, then, there developed a three-fold social division of labour, between capital farmers, family farmers, and farm workers, and this served to emphasize the geographical division of labour, and to make the countries all the more sharply distinguished the one from the other. They differed in their agricultural systems, in their livestock and in their social structure. They were entities of themselves and they were also members one of another. Each had its own character and its own way of life.

There was a group of what might loosely be classified as downland countries. The *Chalk Country* was largely composed of the billowing downs and sheltered valleys of Wessex. The hill country and the southern parts of Wiltshire referred to by Aubrey and others were a part of this. The *Southdown Country* lay on and around the South Downs from the sea westwards as far as the River Lavant and Chichester, and in the central and southern part of the Isle of Wight. The *Northdown Country* consisted of the North Downs and their minor extensions, the Isle of Thanet, the Canterbury and Maidstone districts, and some associated vales and marshes. The *Chiltern Country* embraced the Chiltern Hills and the East Anglian Heights, together with the Gog Magog Hills and the Brickhills district. The *Northwold Country* was made up of the Wolds north and south of the Humber and some associated marsh and vale lands. The *Oxford Heights Country* was based on the Oxford Heights as they extended south-westwards from that city and included also some adjacent lands in the Vale of White Horse.

The soils in all these countries tended to be light and often shallow loams, but some tracts of clay-with-flints were found in most of them. It might be said that whereas in the rest of these countries chalk hills stood above the clay, in the Northdown and Chiltern Countries, to a large extent, clay soils stood on the chalk. However, all these countries had almost completely absorbent bases, which in the Oxford Heights Country was composed of soft limestone and everywhere else of pure chalk. This made the soils warm and dry.

Over so great an area there was obviously a good deal of variation in climate, which was somewhat drier in the Chiltern and Northdown and cooler in the Northwold Country. But the climature (which was the combined effect of soils, base and climate), though more backward than in neighbouring plains and vales, was almost uniformly favourable for both corn and sheep. These were, indeed, great sheep-and-corn countries, where most of the land was either sheep-pasture, or tillage that was folded by the sheep throughout the year, excepting only a few of the worst nights.

Since these were all corn countries, large capital farms had the advantage of small family ones. In the Chiltern and Northdown Countries, which were the best for corn, capital farms already commanded the field. Elsewhere they were still engaged in gaining it, and as long as part-time and family farms persisted in some numbers, so long did common fields survive. It was only these little farmers who needed common fields, and where common fields had been done away with, which was the position in most of the Chiltern and almost all of the Northdown Country, such farmers found their opportunities severely limited. The capital farms either had their lands in severalty already or were actively engaged in extricating them from the common fields.

The shallower the hill soils, the more prevalent was shifting and temporary cultivation. It was found to some extent in all these countries, but hardly at all in the Northdown and Chiltern and most of all in the Northwold Country. Generally speaking, the more extensive the common fields, the less productive and the more rigid and uniform were the prevailing field-courses. Two-field courses, in which corn crops alternated with bare fallow, were followed in many widely scattered places, but were only of the first importance in the Northwold Country. Three-field courses, where winter corn was followed by spring corn and then by bare fallow, occurred in the better lands of the Northwold Country, and were widely adopted in the Chalk, Southdown and Oxford Heights Countries. In the heavy-soiled common fields in the woodlands on the backs of the Chilterns, the three-field course was arranged in the plain-country way, by which a fine tilth was followed by a crop of rough grains and pulse on the inverted stubbles. Severalty, of course, made a good farmer better and a bad one worse. Wherever capital farms in severalty held sway, and above all in the Northdown Country, the field-courses were much more flexible and the fallows were usually sown with crops, resulting in a more or less continuous round of corn and pulse crops. In the Northdown Country the great fallow crop was 'podware', by which was meant various mixtures of tares and peas. Similar crops elsewhere were often called 'horsemeat', because used for that purpose.

In all these countries the farmers expected to maximize their profits by concentrating on the production of wheat and barley. Then the various sidelines made useful additions to farm in-comes: store sheep in the Chalk Country; fruit and hops in the Northdown Country; saffron in the Chiltern Country; and, everywhere, wool.

Shire horses, mainly imported from other parts of England, were generally used, two or three to a plough-team in the Chalk Country, three or four in the Northwold Country, two, or two or three pairs in the Chiltern Country, and so on (*plates 23, 24, 25*). Family farmers generally, and in the Oxford Heights Country many capital farmers also, employed ox-teams (*plate 23*) or mixed teams of oxen led by horses. Otherwise cows were usually kept only for domestic dairies and liquid milk supplies, and the cattle themselves were largely imported from neighbour-ing plain and vale countries. The Southdown Country, for instance, stocked mainly 'Sussex' cattle that hailed from the High Weald via the Wealden Vales.

The Chalk Country farmers bred and reared their native sheep both for themselves and for sale to the Northdown and Chiltern Countries. Thanks to their extensive sheep-downs and their rich meadows, the Chalk Country men were well placed for raising sheep, but they had fewer forage crops to fatten them on, and so were only too pleased to sell them as stores. Northdown and

Chiltern farmers, therefore, did not bother to breed and rear sheep for themselves, but economized by buying Chalk Country wethers. The only exceptions to this general rule were that a few Romney Marsh sheep were overwintered in the Northdown Country and in the north of the Chiltern Country some East Anglian sheep were stocked. These Old Chalk Country sheep are sometimes called 'Old Wiltshire', 'Old Hampshire', and so on, according to which county the speaker happens to be in, and were the ancestors of what are now called the 'Wiltshire Horn' sheep. They were bred specifically for folding on the arable, and for walking to and fro, not for standing still. The sheep-masters paid little or no attention to improving the carcass for the butcher and looked only for the hardiness the sheep needed to pick up a living on a close-fed down, to walk two or three miles for its keep and then to carry its dung back the same distance to the fold on the tillage. This was a big, hefty animal. It had a large head, big eyes, long, arched face, wide nostrils, wide, deep chest, straight back, long sturdy legs, and horns which in both sexes fell back behind the ears. With its long but relatively light frame, this was a naturally active and agile animal that could pass with ease up and down the often steep hills that separated the nightly fold from the daily pasture. It was a greedy feeder and slow to fatten, but could eventually be brought to a good weight of mutton (*plate 13*). The Southdown Country also had its own native breed. The Old Southdowns were polled, in other words, naturally hornless, and black-faced, with a tuft of white wool on their foreheads. They were about the same size as the Old Chalk Country sheep and just as active and agile. They had high shoulders, sharp backs and strong legs. The Old Northwold breed was similar again and so was the 'Nott' or hornless breed that belonged to the Oxford Heights Country. One thing all these sheep had in common was that they were hardy, intelligent, arable breeds and well able to endure folding throughout the year. A second characteristic they all shared was that they bore fleeces of about two pounds of short, fine, wool that was carded and used in the woollen clothing industry.

The five heathland countries were in many ways similar to the downland ones. The *Norfolk Heathlands* lay on and around the Norfolk Edge and the Cromer Ridge. A broad gap between the East Anglian Heights and the Norfolk Edge gave rise to the *Breckland*, whose core was a wide expanse of poor heathland. The *Sandlings Country* consisted essentially of the sandy heaths that lay near the seacoast and between the estuaries of Suffolk. The *Blackheath Country* was made up largely of the black sands of Bagshot, Ascot and Bisley heaths, Maidenhead Thicket, and Windsor and Alice Holt forests. The *Poor Soils Country* included the isles of Purbeck and Portland, the heathlands to the north, and the New Forest.

All these countries had mostly poor, thin, sandy or gravelly soils on bases of absorbent chalk or sand, with the chief exception that the Norfolk Heathlands and the Sandlings Country had also many rich coastal marshlands. In all of them a climate markedly favourable to cereal crops was offset by the dryness and poverty of most of the soil, much of which in the Breckland and the Blackheath Country was hardly better than a blowing sand. The old joke about the Breckland farmer who said his farm was either in Norfolk or Suffolk, depending which way the wind happened to be blowing, exaggerates only to make a good point. All these dry sandy soils were much better for rye than for wheat and gave rise to pastures of ling and heather rather than of grass. But this same dryness was ideal for folding sheep on the arable throughout the year. Sheep-and-corn husbandry was the universal practice, except in the royal forests, where sheep were excluded to make room for the deer, with the result that only the most miserable sort of husbandry was possible. Otherwise, poor as the soils were, by dint of folding sheep upon them, they could be forced to yield good crops of rye, barley and oats. And when they were not cropped, these same lands grew heather and other herbage suitable for sustaining large sheepflocks. Fertility varied considerably according to the depth of the soil and to the amount of rich pasture and meadow attached to the farms. On both counts the Sandlings Country was the most, and the Blackheath the least fortunate.

These, then, were all cereal countries, but ones where good

crops could be gained only in return for heavy investments in folding sheep. Capital farms, therefore, generally had the advantage of family ones, and predominated over them in the Norfolk Heathlands, the Breckland and the Sandlings Country. In the Poor Soils Country (less the New Forest) capital farms were ousting family ones much as they were in the neighbouring Chalk Country. In this and some other respects, indeed, the one country may be considered as a vastly inferior version of the other. Only in the Blackheath Country and the New Forest did the family farmer come into his own, and this largely in subsistence husbandry on land that working and gentlemen farmers considered unfit for their purposes. Corresponding to these differences in social structure, the common fields were of very small extent in the Sandlings Country, modest in dimensions in the Norfolk Heathlands and the Breckland, moderate in the Poor Soils Country, and loomed large only in the Blackheath Country. The capital farms were mostly in severalty even where they were not enclosed.

A great deal of the land allowed only temporary and shifting cultivation. The common practice was to take in plots of heathland and sow them, chiefly to rye, for a few years, and then leave them to go back to the heath again. In the Norfolk Heathlands and the Breckland, these plots or 'brecks' were close-folded twice in rapid succession in order to force a crop. In the Blackheath Country the heaths could be made to bear rye only by paring and burning the vegetation and sowing seed in the mixed ashes and soil. All the same, varying proportions of these countries were cultivated permanently. The arable enclosures of the Norfolk Heathlands, the Breckland and the Sandlings Country, and what few there were in the Blackheath and Poor Soils Countries, were alternated between runs of corn crops and short leys of indifferent grass whose chief function was to put some heart into the land. In the permanent common fields of the three East Anglian countries, various field-courses were employed, ranging between the two-field one and complicated five- and six-field ones. In the Poor Soils and Blackheath Countries, two-field courses were the most usual.

F

The capital farmers, especially the East Anglian ones, were large-scale growers for the market, specialising in rye and barley. What dairies were kept were generally small and for domestic purposes only, but the Sandlings Country took advantage of its rich marshlands to produce much cheese and butter from large herds of dun cows. Thanks to the marshes along the coast, too, the Norfolk Heathlands fatted some stock on grass. The plough-teams were everywhere formed of horses, with two or three to the team in the Norfolk Heathlands and the Breckland and usually one or two in the Sandlings Country. All these East Anglian countries stocked chiefly their native punches, which were the only specialized farm horses in the kingdom. The farmers of the Sandlings Country utilized their marshlands to make the breeding and rearing of these punches one of their chief objects.

All these eastern countries, too, stocked sheep of the native East Anglian breed. These had black or mottled faces, long, slender bodies, long legs, and horns that were spiral in the rams and straight in ewes and wethers. The Poor Soils Country used Chalk Country sheep and the Blackheath Country had its own small, mean, ill-formed 'heathcroppers' to match its stunted cows and horses. All these breeds of sheep made good mutton when fatted, but were kept primarily for their work in the fold. The East Anglians, like the Chalk Country sheep, gave two-pound fleeces of short, fine wool to be carded for the manufacture of woolen cloth, and the 'heathcroppers' similar but lighter ones.

Next we may consider two countries where the fatting of lambs was at least equally as important as the folding of sheep for corn. The *South Seacoast Country* extended along the coast between Brighton, Southampton and Poole, and to the north of the Isle of Wight; and the small district that formed the *Petworth Country* occupied a break in the escarpment of the South Downs. The South Seacoast Country had large tracts of deep loams and smaller ones of poorer and shallower soils. It also included a narrow ridge of chalky soils on Portsdown and some rich coastal marshes. The Petworth Country had a wide range of soils from stiff clays to poor sands. But in both the base was mostly absorbent and largely chalky. Both countries, too, had warm climates, and the South Seacoast Country was exceptionally favoured in that it generally inclined towards the sun and enjoyed extra warmth from its rays, so that its climature was excellent for cereals.

Once again the cost advantage was with capital farms, which occupied most of the South Seacoast Country and were on the ascendant in the Petworth Country. Both had originally been largely champion and common field, but already the former was mostly enclosed and the latter rapidly enclosing. In neither country was there much in the way of regular and general field-courses and crop-rotations. The tendency was to develop more or less continuous crops of corn and pulses and severely to restrict bare fallows, while alternating corn and grass in many of the fields. The South Seacoast Country had much powerful wheat land and wheat was the chief crop; but in the Petworth Country barley and rye were each grown much more than wheat. Domestic dairies and horse-teams were kept and the South Seacoast farmers with marshland fattened some bullocks. The chief stock, however, was of 'Dorset' house-lamb sheep. Ewes were bought at Dorchester in the autumn when they were already with lamb. In December they usually gave birth to twins, which they suckled until fat enough for the butcher. During this period the ewes were highly fed on grass and tare hay and cereals and later folded and fed on rye and winter vetches. Their suckling completed, the ewes in their turn were fatted for the butcher, making way for fresh drafts of in-lamb ewes.

The *Cotswold Country* comprised the Cotswold, Southwold, Stroudwater, Edge and Dundry hills and associated lands. Here the soils were largely stony or gravelly and stood on a base of almost impervious limestone. This, combined with a relatively damp climate, made it unsafe to fold sheep on the tillage in the wet winter months, so that they had then to be housed in cotes, which gave the hills their name. But in summer time these same sheep were assiduously folded, going upon the extensive sheep pastures by day and on the tillage by night. The Cotswold was a champion, sheep-and-corn country despite the fact that it was not wholly suited to such a role. As such, it favoured the growth of capital farms at the expense of family ones and hence severalty rather than common fields. Many large common fields still existed in the sixteenth century, but as they created their large farms by the merger of small ones, the capital farmers took the earliest opportunity of getting rid of common rights.

Until the seventeenth century the field-course that generally prevailed was a simple two-field one, with the emphasis on spring corn and barley rather than on winter corn and wheat. Except on the lower and easterly slopes, where the soils were more favourable to grass, dairying was confined to the satisfaction of purely domestic requirements. Both horses and oxen were put to the plough, the former tending to replace the latter. The native sheep were the Old Cotswolds, a polled breed with small faces, white skins, long, spare, big-boned frames, square hulks and big buttocks. Thanks to the sparseness of their feed and a combination of rigorous summer folding and protective cotting in winter, they grew what for arable sheep were the large three-pound fleeces of excellent, fine, short, carding wool for the woollen industry.

If the Cotswold Country was only half suited to sheep-and-corn husbandry, there were two others that were quite unsuited to it and yet where it was nevertheless practised. Here sheep were pastured by day and folded on the tillage at night, not because this system presented farmers with their greatest advantage and gave them the wares from which they could get the best profits, but because the people who occupied the land concerned themselves only with subsistence and existence. This was the lamentable position in both the *Midland Plain* and the *Vale of Pickering* in the middle ages and the early sixteenth century and, decreasingly, for some time afterwards. Both these countries had mostly heavy, cold, wet soils on impervious and retentive bases, so that sheep-folding was dangerous in the winter months. Both, too, were maintained as champion countries by purely artificial means, when they were much more suited to enclosures. In both, too, the greater part of the land was in relatively unproductive common fields and backward part-time and family farms. The usual field-course in both was the plain-country three-field one, under which the land was first brought to a fine tilth for small crops of winter corn and larger ones of spring barley, then the stubble was ploughed once for crops of rough grains and pulses, and finally barefallowed. This was mere subsistence farming, and persisted only because the farmers in the Vale of Pickering had not yet found a suitable niche for themselves in wider markets, and because those in the Midland Plain were so wedded to subsistence farming that they made no attempt even to seek a solution of their transportation problems. Their roads were largely too deep and miry for heavy road haulage, the navigable rivers mostly flowed away from the markets, and canals were unthought of.

As we shall see later, the Pickering farmers solved their difficulties by going over to grass dairying, and already in the Middle Ages some kind of a solution had been found for the problems of the Midland Plain when, in some parts and places, the little farms were vacated and their lands thrown into enclosures of permanent grass in the hands of graziers who made it their business to produce fat stock. The land here suited grass very well and the fat stock could easily be walked to market in the summer months. And this was the first way the Midland Plain was drawn into the division of labour. The graziers imported cattle in spring time from the Lancashire Plain and elsewhere, but they maintained their own breed of pasture sheep after having derived it, probably, from that of the Fen Country. The 'Warwick' or 'Old Leicester' pasture sheep in the main body of the plain were heavy, polled animals, with big bones, long, thick legs, slaw feet and large, loose frames. As compared with the fallow sheep imported and used by the common-field farmers, these pasture sheep had twice the weight both of flesh and of fleece, and their fleeces yielded not carding wool for the woollen industry, but combing wool for the manufacture of worsteds. In the northern limb of the plain, in the vales of York and Stockton, the Teeswater pasture sheep were quite similar, and the two strains were considerably intermixed.

High Suffolk was well watered and had deep and fertile soils, as well as a climate congenial to corn. Indeed, this country, with the Woodland, was the part of the world which best suited the cultivation of cereals. Despite this, however, High Suffolk farmers chose to engage in a mixture of corn-growing and dairying, since most of the neighbouring countries were excellent for corn, whereas only High Suffolk, and the marshy parts of the Sandlings Country, were suited to the dairy. High Suffolk thus shared in the corn-growing of eastern England, but specialized in producing butter and cheese from cows fed on grass in the summer months and on straw and hay in the winter. High Suffolk farmers were quite unlike the little dairy-graziers found in the Cheese Country and elsewhere in western England. They were complete farmers, mostly working farmers with large farms laid out in enclosed fields of convertible land that was sometimes laid down from corn to grass and sometimes ploughed up from grass for corn. The herds, too, far exceeded the capacity of a single family to look after them, even supposing that the wives and daughters would have so demeaned themselves, for they commonly numbered fifty, sixty or more cows. Great plough-teams of four or five punch horses were kept and the farmers were among the most expert corn-growers in the kingdom, but the crops of corn, great though they were, failed to match those of grass. When they had finished making their hay, the farmers had as much as one tenth of their working capital tied up in it. Rather more cheese was made than butter, and this cheese was of two sorts. There was a peerless cream cheese, and a hard cheese, jocularly known as 'bang'. This 'bang' was said to be 'so hard that pigs grunt at it, dogs bark at it, and none dare bite it' and was supposed to mock 'the weak effort of the bending blade'. But it kept better than the cream cheese, was much eaten by the poorer sort, and was unequalled for the provisioning of ships. The native dun cows, universally stocked, were remarkable for being the only polled breed and no less for their excellence in milking. They were large by contemporary standards, with well-knit, long bodies, broad foreheads, deep sides and great milk-bags.

The *Woodland* had soils and climate similar to those of High

Suffolk, but was less well endowed with wet meadows; a fact that helped to persuade the gentlemen and working farmers who occupied most of the land to devote it to corn, and, above all, to wheat. The fields were enclosed and convertible to and from corn and grass, but the grass leys were short-lived and were valued more for the improvement they wrought in the soil than for their immediate produce, for little interest was taken in any livestock beyond the great teams of punches.

East Norfolk was unique among farming countries on account of its great uniformity of sandy loams on beds of sand. Only the broadland district had heavier soils. In comparison with the rest of East Anglia the climate was windy, cool and damp, but East Norfolk was still highly suited to corn-growing. By the early sixteenth century an ancient sheep-and-corn husbandry similar to that of the Norfolk Heathlands had been displaced by a system of enclosed farming that combined corn crops with the stall-feeding of bullocks for the butcher. This was a business carried on in large farms by wealthy capital farmers. The country had its own breed of beef cattle, not unlike diminutive Herefords, and thought to have been derived, at least partly, from that race. Native punch horses, too, were generally stocked, two or three going to make up a plough-team.

The *Vale of Taunton Deane* was another striking instance of early specialization. This was a small, woodland country bounded and sheltered by the Blackdown Hills and Exmoor, and it developed a husbandry utterly unlike those of its neighbours. With its excellent, deep sandy soils or heavy loams and its mild and serene climate, it was the best of the few western countries suitable for corn-growing. This gave its farmers a wonderful opportunity they were quick to take advantage of. Making the most of their enclosed fields by converting them to and from corn and grass, utilizing expensive horse teams, and cultivating wheat and other cereals with immense care and labour, they made their country the granary of the west, a veritable 'land of Canaan' and the 'paradise of England'. The yields of wheat were prodigious and of so high a quality that they were bought for seed by the farmers of the Chalk and Southdown Countries.

The *Vale of Evesham* was another much favoured and improved western country. Its soils were chiefly deep, fertile loams and its base mostly retentive. It enjoyed warm summers, mild winters and a moderate rainfall, and was generally suited to both corn and grass. Sheep could be folded only in the summer months, and that the common fields were so heavily manured was due largely to the herds of dairy cows kept everywhere. The farmers had made their common fields so productive that they had been able to adopt a four-field course of the plain-country type, where a year of fine tilth was followed by two successive breach crops on the upturned stubbles and then by a year of fallow. The fact that these fields were so rich and productive discouraged and postponed their enclosure, and this in turn made this a country suitable for small farmers who could hope to stay in business by intensifying the cultivation of the richer and more easily worked soils by means of their own, largely hand labour. At the same time there also developed many large severalty farms with most of their fields enclosed, where the land was sometimes ploughed for corn and at others laid down for grass. One way and another, cereal cultivation was well combined with rich grasslands for dairying. The cheese made was dubbed 'Warwick' and sold widely. This country was the nursery of the Old Gloucester breed of cows. These had horns of middling length, being in this respect about halfway between the long and shorthorn breeds. They were mostly dark red or brown, with black muzzles and legs and white rumps and tails. These pied cattle were also good for beef, and more than a few were fattened here, but they were prized chiefly for their milking qualities.

Going northwards the chain of western dairy countries was resumed in the *Cheshire Cheese Country*, which consisted essentially of the Vale Royal, the vales of Warrington, Shrewsbury, Clwyd and Montgomery and the district of the Wiches. This was a moist country with soils derived from clay, silt and sand, standing on impervious bases, and giving rise to a sour herbage best suited to cheese production. At the same time, however, it was better suited to corn-growing than any country to the west or north of it, and the wheatsheaf was more in evidence here than anywhere else in the north-west. The mixed-dairy farmers regularly ploughed up their fields of grass in order both to secure corn crops and to encourage that growth of young and nutritious grass demanded by their herds of Lancashire longhorn cows. The scale of business varied all the way from the smallest family farm to the largest capital one, but the balance of advantage lay with the gentlemen and working farmers who cultivated substantial crops of corn with their ox or mixed teams and grazed herds of up to a hundred cows. This was the largest cheese-dairy country in the kingdom, with tens of thousands of cows devoted to producing farmhouse 'Cheshire' cheese.

The rest of the western, woodland, dairy countries were less suited to corn and specialized in dairy-grazing conducted by small family farmers who took only a casual interest in tilling the land. They mostly aimed to ensure against downright famine and to grow what straw they needed for their farms, and otherwise to restrict ploughing to the minimum. Side by side with the dairy-men, however, there were in all these countries some few graziers who occupied themselves in fattening sheep and cattle for the butcher. As the supplies of grain from outside became ampler and surer, the common fields, which had never grown very large, and where plain-country courses were followed, were more and more abandoned in favour of enclosed fields that were little and seldom ploughed.

The vales of Blackmoor, Glastonbury, Ilminster, Glamorgan and Marshwood, and the western part of the Vale of Wardour, made up the *Butter Country*. The grasses here were best suited, in most parts, to milk for buttermaking. A notable feature here was that the hills and slopes between which the vales were spread were the nurseries of the house-lamb or 'Dorset' breed of sheep we met in the South Seacoast and Petworth Countries.

Between the folds of the downs and wolds and the Oxford Heights lay the vales of the *Cheese Country*, most of which was made up of John Aubrey's 'North Wilts'. Here the grass was sourer and mostly suited to cheese, which went by the names of 'Marlborough', because sold there, or 'Gloucester', because it resembled that made in the *Vale of Berkeley*. Indeed, the chief differences between these two countries were that the Cheese Country farmers made cheese in winter also, from hay, which was something their competitors in the Vale of Berkeley could not aspire to; and that the former preferred Lancashire longhorn cows and the latter Old Gloucesters.

Lastly, the *Western Waterlands* made a dairy-grazing country with a difference. It contained extensive areas of fens or moors in the Brue, Brent and Parrett marshes, the Sedgemoors, the Clevedon and Nailsea flats, and the Wentlloog and Caldicot levels, together with the main settlements on the uplands of the Isle of Avalon, Brent Knoll, the Bleadon, Polden and Mendip Hills and elsewhere. These moors had largely been drained into good summerground, which was all the farmers asked of them, seeing that it was grass and not corn that they most wanted. Only the upland soils were tilled to any extent, and then largely in common fields, and even with sheep-folding in summer. As the amount of marsh and grass so much exceeded that of tillage, fertilizers were produced in plenty and good corn crops were taken. It is noteworthy that the wheat grown in the Polden Hills, for example, was of the very best quality and much sought after for the seed; and yet the farmers showed little interest in expanding their corn acreages. Instead, they found their greatest advantages in raising and fattening sheep and lambs of the house-lamb race, in breeding and rearing shire horses, and in keeping herds of Old Gloucester cattle, partly to be fattened, mostly to be milked for the manufacture mainly of butter, but in the Brue Marshes of the high-quality cheese called 'Cheddar'.

The *Wealden Vales* formed another deep, enclosed woodland country, but one that specialized in meat production to the virtual exclusion of dairying. The soils here were mostly weak, woodland clays, and though they were being greatly improved by marling, and increased in number and size by the progressive clearance of woodlands, the fields could bear neither corn nor grass for long periods and had to be chopped and changed between one and the other, with the chief object of improving the grass. Both cultivation and improvement, and buying cattle of the 'Sussex' breed from the High Weald to draw the ploughs and stock the fields, demanded big capital outlays and it is hardly surprising that the occupation of these vales should have gravitated into the hands of gentlemen and working farmers.

The country here called *Romney Marsh* in fact included also Walland and Denge marshes, Broomhill, Rother, Upper, Brede, Wittersham, Guldeford, Mountney, Pett, and Pevensey levels, and Shirley Moor, along with the Isle of Oxney and the barren sandhills to the west of them. The marshes were all rich clay or silt loams. They were heavy and humid in summer and cold and black in winter. 'Evil in winter, grievious in summer, and never good' was hardly an unduly harsh summing up of the climate of 'the windy levels spread about the gates of Rye'. This was a country almost entirely regained from the sea, and mainly in the hands of well-to-do graziers who preferred to live high and dry in the uplands and leave the oversight of their flocks and herds to resident marshlookers. These graziers sometimes grew a little corn, but were above all interested in producing fat stock, and then mainly fat mutton. 'Sussex' cattle, and many other and remoter breeds, were brought here to be fattened, especially in Pevensey Level, in the 'pastures wide and lone where the red oxen browse'. Elsewhere, and generally, the scarcity of running water made the marshes more suitable for sheep, and in particular to the native Romney Marsh breed. Like all pasture sheep, these were big, polled animals. They had long legs, deep paunches, thick necks and heavy fleeces of very long, semi-lustrous combing wool, well suited to all but the finest worsteds. These were extremely hardy sheep, else they would never have survived marsh winters, and they fattened well.

The *Saltings Country* had much in common with Romney Marsh, but only half of it could claim to have been wrested from the sea. The uplands where the farmers lived were here both more extensive and more fertile. All the soils were wet and cold by nature, and the upland onces, being mostly heavy clays lying on beds of impenetrable clay, were numbered among the most intractable in the kingdom. But a favourable climate encouraged their expensive and laborious cultivation, with strong horse teams, for excellent crops of wheat and other cereals. The marshlands, too, were much ploughed and sown to mustard and cole-seed as well as to corn. At the same time, the uplands were as good for dairy cows and fat cattle as the marshlands were for mutton, so what with one thing and another a rich and varied husbandry was conducted by wealthy gentlemen and working farmers.

The greatest marshland area formed the mass of the *Fen Country*. There were fresh peat fens inland and salt silt ones on the coast, so that settlement was possible only in upland places like the Isle of Ely, on the silt ridge north of the peat fens, and on the bordering 'highlands' (*plate 15*). These peat fens gave rise to fertile black fenmoulds; the silty soils of the coastal marshes were not much inferior; and at the junction of the silt and the peat were the incomparable skirt soils or highly organic silty clay loams. All the main areas of settlement, therefore, were mixed-farming districts, with common fields and sheep-folds upon them in the summer or enclosed fields of grass and corn crops. The fens that dominated the entire country ensured its farmers a superabundance of pasture, hay, and farmyard manure, and this made the surrounding arable far more fertile than it would otherwise have been. Highly productive field-courses were widely possible, and the best of the lands were often subjected to a continuous round of hemp, flax, grain, pulse and other crops. In the arable farming based on the towns, on the islands, and highlands, economies of scale gave the advantage to capital farms; but this still left ample scope for a multitude of little men to eke out their livings by fishing, fowling and grazing in the depth of the fens. But with every drainage of fens to winterground, capital farmers took over the land, made it arable and cultivated oats, cole-seed and other crops. Thus in various parts almost every possible objective was followed by one kind of occupier or another: grazing for the butter-dairy, beef and mutton; the raising of foals from the brood shire mares that were the usual work horses; the breeding and rearing of sheep; the growing of corn; and the cultivation of industrial or semi-industrial crops like hemp, flax and cole-seed. This last was fed to sheep before being left to go to seed for crushing in the oil-mills (*plate 7*). The Fen Country was noted for its fine race of pasture sheep, which was called 'Norfolk' or 'Lincolnshire' according to whether it happened to be in the Marshland or in some other part of the country. These Fen sheep were allied to and often interbred with the Midland pasture sheep; but the Fen sheep were the larger of the two. They had the longest carcasses and legs of any in England and were so big that a fen ram endangered the life of a Midland pasture ewe in lambing. Fen sheep were inured to wet ground and fattened up well on either grass or green crops. They bore extremely heavy fleeces, which in wethers often weighed as much as ten pounds, but with the notable exception of those from the better-drained Marshland district (*plate 14*), their combing wool was not yet of the first quality.

The farmers of the *Lancashire Plain* found their best opening in the rearing of longhorn cattle. From the North Country, and especially from the Craven district and the upper Ribble valley, they bought calves that they then reared and resold to graziers in the Midland Plain or farmers in the Cheshire Cheese Country and elsewhere in central and southern England. These cattle were excellent for all purposes, whether for fattening, for milking, or for ploughing and haulage. The cows were splendid milkers, when milk solids were required and not just gallons of watery fluid, and were invaluable where the grass was suited to cheese, because their milk gave so much curd. The bullocks could be rapidly fattened to a great weight of first-class beef, or yoked and worked, for they were strong, large-built, big-boned and soundly constituted. The Lancashire Plain farmers excelled in rearing these magnificent beasts on the fresh young grass of their temporary leys. As a necessary joint-product they grew some corn in the short periods for which almost all the land was sooner or later put under the plough. But neither the rich, black fenmoulds, nor the sandy or clayey loams were highly suited to corn-growing in this rather cool, moist climate. Nor were the grasslands usually rich enough for fattening much stock or dry enough to warrant making a big business of sheep. And then, being rather remote from the most populous parts of the realm, it was handy to be able to sell wares that could take themselves to market. Everything thus conspired to impel farmers to their chosen speciality. As big sums needed to be disbursed for calves and as the proportion of arable land was high, large farms generally had the advantage over small ones and rearing was mostly conducted on a vast scale. Many farms had constantly between one and two hundred head of cattle and the largest ones between two and four thousand. Effort was thus concentrated on the mass rearing of longhorns.

The *Vales of Hereford* went into a rather similar line of business. The climate, while not markedly different in other ways, was somewhat sunnier and better for cereals, as well as being good for fruit and hops. Although fenmoulds were absent, the variety of soils was otherwise not entirely dissimilar, and the relatively large and compact area of hot, sandy, and gravelly 'ryelands' gave a better habitat for sheep. These vales were the home of the famous Ryeland breed, which were bred and reared here and employed in a peculiar form of sheep-and-corn husbandry, where the sheep were not folded on the tillage, but cotted by night throughout the year and their muck carted out to the fields. These Ryelands were small-boned, shapely sheep, with off-white skins, and being polled, were all the more suited to what was a largely enclosed country. Cotting checked carcass growth and improved the quality but lessened the quantity of the fleeces, which often weighed only one pound and seldom as much as two even in the best wethers. This lightness was compensated, however, by the high prices fetched by the fine, short, silky, carding wool, which was generally regarded as the best of its kind. Cotting, too, both preserved the Ryelands from footrot and made them too delicate to withstand the rigours of the fold. Nevertheless, they had the ability to get a living on the poorest pasture, and truly deserved, as Sir Joseph Banks said, 'a niche in the temple of famine'. The farmers' grand object, even in the ryeland district, was the breeding and rearing of Hereford cattle. These massive, middle-horn beasts were reckoned second to none for beef and were sold widely as stores to farmers in midland, southern, and eastern England, who, unlike those in these vales, had the pastures to fatten them on. The breeding and rearing of Ryeland sheep and Hereford cattle on mainly temporary pastures was combined with corn-growing and fruit and hop cultivation. Such a mixed husbandry was best conducted by men of means and a large part of the land was occupied by gentlemen and working farmers.

We now come to the hill-farming countries, which generally speaking were unfit for commercial corn-growing, dairying or meat production. Their soils were mostly unable to bear the best either of corn or of grass, and their climates were likewise unfavourable to crops in varying degrees. Permanent cultivation was rarely possible and it usually took the paring and burning of the turf to bring the land into even temporary cultivation for short successions of crops. The best aim for farmers to set themselves was thus the raising of sheep, cattle, and ponies, and this suited family farmers who could do what little ploughing was required and still devote care and attention to their stock. They were so many Abrahams who dwelt amidst their flocks and herds and lived by the sale of the natural increase they could not hope to keep and feed.

The most and the next most favoured of these countries, respectively the *West Country* and *Wales*, were able both to breed and to rear sheep and middle-horn cattle. The black cattle that attained the greatest stature were usually retained in Wales for ploughing and haulage, and it was the lowest runts rather than the largest oxen that swam the Menai Strait and made up the 'Spanish fleet' that brought silver to the whole country. The red 'Devon' cattle, especially in the favoured South Hams district, were somewhat superior, but in and about the moorlands were likewise coarse and stunted. The sheep in these countries were of mountain or forest types. As a rule, only the rams were horned, all the carcasses were small but made good meat, and the fleeces were poor and hairy, being mostly too short for combing and too long for carding, and so perforce employed in the making of inferior cloths, flannels, knitwear, rugs and carpets. The Dartmoor and Exmoor sheep were like this, and so were most of those in Wales, which had the added disadvantage that they were too

wild to be put into ordinary enclosures and had to be sent into
the moated pastures of the Romney Marsh and the Saltings
Country. Only on the eastern slopes, in and about Kerry Hill,
Clun Forest and Wenlock Edge lived a superior breed of forest
sheep. These 'March' sheep, as they were called, bore good, fine,
short fleeces suitable for woollen clothing. Similarly, in the
South Hams district of the West Country there developed a
large, polled sheep with a fleece of long, curly wool that could
be used in making kerseys, hosiery and worsteds.

The other hill-farming countries were still poorer. In the
North, Peak-Forest, Blackmoors and *High Weald Countries* even
paring and burning could not produce much in the way of crops,
even so lowly as oats, and there was very little grass good enough
to put growing cattle on. The farmers here were thus forced to
live almost solely by selling sheep, calves and in-calvers, and
were, for the most part, as impoverished and backward a lot as
one could expect to meet. And even then we must except from
this general run of petty farmers those uncivilized people who
inhabited the Scottish marches. The North Country bred longhorn cattle in the west and shorthorns in the east, while the
High Weald was the cradle of the hardy, red 'Sussex' or 'Kent'
middlehorns which were so noted for their ability to 'die well'
and 'cut up well'. Over most of the North Country, the sheep
were of a distinct moorland breed, aptly called blackfaces. They
were ill-shaped and with large spiral horns, but their great asset
was that they were able to survive the winter on the open moors.
In the more sheltered Cheviot Hills, there lived a polled, white-
skinned breed which gave wool good enough to be used in rough
tweeds, and in the Lake district that of the Herdwick sheep could
be utilized in coarse Kendal cloths. The rams of this last breed
were noted for their much curved horns. Then, in the relatively
warm and dry soils of the Craven district flourished the Lank
sheep, with large, projecting horns, much twisted on rams and
less so on ewes. These, too, had what, in a mountain sheep, was
esteemed a good fleece. The Peak-Forest sheep were mostly of
the Gritstone type and gave wool that was not unsuitable for
hosiery, but the Sherwood breed here grew somewhat finer

fibres. The Blackmoors Country had a moorland breed of its own, and the High Weald an aboriginal sheep somewhat resembling those of Dartmoor and Exmoor and with a similarly hairy fleece.

It should be added in passing that the Peak-Forest Country, consisting of High Peak, Trawden, Rossendale and Sherwood forests and associated lands, was as much industrial as agricultural, and many of its denizens were part-time farmers with very little in view beyond mere subsistence. The farmers of the Blackmoors Country were mostly whole-timers, but their greatest ambition, likewise, was to live.

Temporary cultivation and subsistence farming were also the general rules in the *North-western* and *North-eastern Lowlands*. It was the measure of the potential superiority of the latter over the former that no one expected anything of the peasants in the North-western Lowlands, whereas those in the North-eastern ones at least merited the despair of surveyors. 'The arable land', said one, 'is a wasted, lean land, for that they are not able to dung it as the same would be.' Another suggested the peasants be encouraged to keep goats in a desperate attempt to break out of the vicious circle of poverty; but it had also to be conceded that even where coal was readily available near the surface, the peasants preferred to tear up and burn the turf that might have fed their beasts and fatted their land.

Lastly, we come to the *Vale of London*. The farmers here had every opportunity to develop production for the market, but largely by means other than agriculture in the ordinary meaning of the word. Since Londoners had no kitchen-gardens, market-gardens sprang up to supply their needs. Since they could not keep domestic dairies, cow-keepers proliferated and the dairymen concentrated on producing liquid milk, cream, and butter, which would command a premium by its freshness. Since most meat could come into London on the hoof, many men were tempted to become either grazing butchers who received fat stock from afar and kept it on grass until required, or producers of veal and house-lamb, which could not foot it and had to be taken to market on horseback. Since the City was as choked with horse

G

carriages then as it is with horseless ones now, many farmers got a good living simply by growing, mowing and selling hay for the stables. In these and other ways, the Vale of London became progressively forced into a suburban way of life.

The Division of Labour and the Growth of Trade

Once it had started, the geographical division of labour fed on itself. Because the Cheese Country specialized in, and so lowered the cost and multiplied the production of cheese, the farmers there were able and anxious to import more cereals and livestock, which in turn allowed them to concentrate more and more on cheese. Conversely, the Chalk Country men could turn their land, labour and capital to best advantage by dropping dairying and specializing more and more on sheep and corn. It was such a growth in the division of labour which, as Adam Smith reminds us, has effected 'the greatest improvement in the productive powers of labour, and the greater part of the skill, dexterity and judgment with which it is anywhere directed or applied'. Equally, it was such division of labour that largely accounted for the different talents possessed by different men. Obviously, Cheese Country farmers became increasingly versed in managing dairy cows and their wives in cheese-making, while Chalk Country men developed parallel expertise in keeping sheep and growing corn.

This division of labour entailed the growth of trade. Trade could not have preceded specialization, because before the very first transaction could take place, the one specialist had to have a superfluity of his speciality that he was willing to trade for the superfluity of someone else's. Trade is thus fostered by specialists to serve their division of labour, and the greater the specialization the greater the trade. The whole of corn, dairy and meat production came to depend, for example, on the livestock trade between countries. The countries where plough-horses were most in demand were rarely the ones where they were bred and reared. Shire horses bred in the Fen Country were reared in the Midland Plain and sold to the downland countries, where they were worked gently and inured to labour before being passed on to carriers and hauliers. The cattle bred in the High Weald had to be sent to the Wealden Vales for rearing and fatting up. Almost everywhere sheep raised in the hill countries were sold to the plains and vales, sometimes to the other side of the kingdom. In most countries the farmers grew at least a little corn, if only to guard against the mischance of harvest failures elsewhere and consequent famines. There were, of course, many corn-deficient countries, but this was less because they could not grow corn than because the farmers had made them corn-deficient on purpose, in order that they could have a surplus of something else to sell in exchange for corn and other commodities. Many countries concentrated on corn-growing, but they nearly all specialized in cultivating different cereals, or different varieties, grades and qualities of the same cereal, or in growing the same crop in a different way, harvesting it at a different time, or marketing it for a different purpose. The dairy countries, too, specialized to the utmost degree, and then exchanged their special products with one another. Thus the Cheese and Butter Countries bought each other's wares. Many countries produced grass meat, but East Norfolk and the Fen Country could add winter beef and mutton. As for the trade in wool, to unravel all its intricacies would be a study in itself. Suffice it to say that hardly any country utilized much of the wool it grew, but sent it to be distributed to various places all over the kingdom. A Swedish visitor to this island, by name of Kalm, put it in a nutshell when he remarked, with evident surprise, that each country specialized in a few crops and left the rest to be grown by others.

Thanks to the social and geographical division of labour, an extensive range of farm produce was offered to consumers. Different kinds of grass cheese came from the Cheese and Cheshire Cheese Countries, the Vale of Berkeley, High Suffolk, the Western Waterlands, and the Vale of Evesham; hay and winter cheeses from the Cheese Country and High Suffolk; grass butters from the Western Waterlands, the Fen and Butter Countries, and High Suffolk; grass beeves and muttons from the Midland Plain, the Wealden Vales, Romney Marsh, and elsewhere;

fat lambs from the South Seacoast and Petworth Countries;
corned beef from East Norfolk and cole-seed mutton from the
Fen Country; wheats from the Woodland, South Seacoast and
Saltings Countries, and the Vale of Taunton Deane, and so on;
barley from the Norfolk Heathlands, the Chalk and Northdown
countries, among others. Yet other fare was provided by the
table fruit of the Northdown and Chiltern Countries, and the
vales of Evesham and London; the hares of the Chalk Country;
the rabbits of the Northwold Country, the Norfolk Heathlands,
and the Breckland; the freshwater fish of the Blackheath Country;
the saffron (*plate 9*) of the Chiltern Country and the liquorice of
Pontefract; the wild fowl (and the mustard) of the Fen and
Saltings Countries; the geese of the Western Waterlands; the
turkeys of East Norfolk and the Sandlings Country. Bacon and
pork came from all the dairying countries, for the pig was tied
to the cow's tail, for the sake of the whey and so on, as in modern
Denmark. Thirsts were quenched, if not from home-brews, then
by the beers and ales of the Northdown, Southdown, Chalk,
Sandlings and other countries, or by ciders and perries from the
West Country, the Vales of Hereford, and the Vales of Evesham
and Taunton Deane.

Capitalistic Economy

Each and every increase in the specializations that had developed,
and were still developing, between the different countries, was
accompanied by the expansion of trade between them, and no
less by the increasingly capitalistic nature of their production as
a whole. Consider, for example, the successive transactions
required to put beef on Londoners' tables. The North Country
farmers, who bred the longhorn calves, sold them to rearers
in the Lancashire Plain. These in time sold grown steers, directly
or indirectly, to Midland or other graziers, who disposed of them
when fat to grazing butchers, who kept them till required by the
carcass butchers, for eventual disposal to the cutting butchers or
meat purveyors. Think of what was needed for Northdown barley
to be brewed into beer. Chalk Country farmers had first to breed,
doctor and rear wether sheep and then sell them at Weyhill or

some other fair. When the wethers arrived in the Northdown
Country, they were folded on the arable for barley, some of
which would prove to be of malting quality. This malt had then
to be brought together with hops grown and picked in the
Northdown Country. But the barley would not have been sown
in the first instance if farmers in the Fen Country had not kept
brood mares and sold foals to be reared in the Midland Plain
before being passed on to the Northdown Country. Many other
examples of chains of similar transactions could be cited, but it
will be clear from what has been said already that sixteenth-
century England was very far from leading a hand-to-mouth
existence. Resources were committed far in advance, to long-
drawnout and roundabout production processes, in anticipation
of consumers' future demands, and the derived and similarly
anticipated demands of other producers, in speculative ventures
involving risky investment. And the livestock trade was already
stamped with the hallmark of capitalistic production: in terms of
volume, value and numbers alike, most of the transactions took
place not with consumers but between different producers of
goods that were as yet unfinished and still awaiting use in the
further processes required before consumers' wants could be
satisfied.

Metropolitan Markets. The countless transactions of an infinitely
intricate commerce could be made only thanks to the services of a
great and growing body of middlemen, who necessarily developed
business ties in great commercial centres. All roads led to London
and all farmers came to look to and watch the London markets,
less because of the city's own consumption than because London
was becoming increasingly the centre and hub of a welter of
metropolitan markets in various kinds of farm produce, both
those ready or almost ready for purchase by consumers and those
still having many stages to pass through before finished products
were obtained. Metropolitan markets handled not only fat stock
but also lean, store cattle, not only wheat to be milled, but also
seed wheat to be sown. In these metropolitan markets, capitalist
farmers (whether family, working or gentleman farmers, or

graziers made no difference) sold their specialized produce privately and wholesale to correspondingly specialist merchants (or merchants' factors), who then redistributed it throughout the whole area populated by the participants in the markets. Just how great these various market areas were depended on: how far the produce was perishable; how easily it could be transported; and on how many and what farmers were participating in the markets concerned. The division of labour between farmers and countries caused trade, and trade made the city grow. The rise and growth of metropolitan markets, and of the great metropolis, was thus the other side of the coin to the division of labour between the various and increasingly differing agricultural countries. Just as, in a previous age, local trade had brought about local pitched markets and market towns, so now trade between farmers in different countries was helping to create metropolitan wholesale markets and the great metropolis itself.

Chapter Four

THE GREAT INVENTIONS

The great inventions of the agricultural revolution were made not at one fell swoop, but step by step and country by country. In any particular country inventions were made that dovetailed in with the existing specialism; and all the inventions were extensions and amplifications of the division of labour already set up. The inventions made some countries and some farmers more specialist than they had been before; but some countries were already so improved that they needed little or no further invention, and still others were beyond help. Since each country adopted the inventions that suited it and each was unique, it is hardly surprising that no single invention was ever universally adopted.

New Farms for Old

One of the most widespread innovations was the construction of capital farms out of petty ones. Whether or not this was accompanied by technical changes, great economies were made. In some instances, old farms were abandoned overnight and the very farmhouses handed over to farm labourers or even demolished. Elsewhere the organization of new capital farms took more the form of consolidating the demesne lands of manors. Instead of letting his demesne out in small parcels to petty tenants or share-croppers, or of having it cultivated by jobbing ploughmen and other lump contractors, the lord or his farmer now ran the whole business himself and employed his own servants and wage-workers in it. Robert Loder of Harwell was only one of many Chalk Country men who reconstructed manorial demesnes in this way. Very little change was to be seen on the surface, but underneath it farming was quite revolutionized. In 1560 such reconstructed demesnes were in a distinct minority in the Chalk Country. A hundred years later they were the majority and accounted for by far the greater part of agricultural production. In another hundred years many townships here had no family farmers left and in the others they were a disappearing race. In Elizabethan times we are told that, 'whereas the ancient tenants kept ploughs, the now cottagers do live only by their day labour', and the same story was repeated over and over again, not only in the Chalk Country, but also in the Southdown, Northwold, Oxford Heights and Cotswold countries and elsewhere. The economies of scale in large farms were of more than theoretical interest: they gave the cutting edge to competition that drove inefficient and wasteful petty farms out of business. In the Northwold Country, for example, we soon hear about 'the poverty and want' of petty farmers forcing them to throw up their little tenancies and keep on only the cottages they needed to live in as servants and labourers.

Up-and-down Husbandry

Although it had recently been adopted to some extent in the extreme north-west, it was only from about 1560 onwards that the Midland Plain as a whole was galvanized by the new introduction of 'up-and-down' husbandry. This is sometimes called 'ley farming', or 'field-grass' or 'convertible' husbandry; but the traditional name is best for what consisted essentially in alternately ploughing grassland *up* for corn *and* laying cornland *down* to grass.

Up-and-down husbandry was not an absolutely new invention. Indeed, it had been practised for some time in the Lancashire Plain, the Cheshire Cheese Country, the Woodland, and High Suffolk. But the general adoption of a specially developed and modified version of up-and-down husbandry throughout the Midland Plain was an invention or innovation of the greatest importance. By 1670 this new husbandry was prevalent in the enclosed farms, which by then included about half the farmland, and had largely out-competed and ousted the old system of having permanent grass and permanent tillage, in the sense that it now out-produced it and contributed well over half the net product of the plain. Then over the next hundred years the older system paled into insignificance.

Up-and-down farming came in to replace permanent tillage, which was mainly in common fields; permanent grass, which was in both common fields and specialist grazing farms; and permanent woodland, large areas of which were now cleared. The old common fields had roughly half their land in permanent grass and half in permanent tillage. Under the new system, after a few meadows and home closes had been set aside, nearly all the land was ploughed, not constantly, of course, but regularly, and in such a way that about a quarter of the farm was devoted to crops of corn and pulse at any one time. The *arable* area was greatly extended, though the amount actually in *tillage* at any any one time was reduced. When grazing farms were broken up, they were treated in much the same way, and then the arable and tillage was all gain. As a whole, therefore, when up-and-down husbandry replaced permanency, the arable was extended and the tillage somewhat reduced.

Bringing in the up-and-down system was by no means an easy task. The old permanent tillage was prone to grass over, and could easily be laid down, but it took between half-a-dozen and a dozen years to produce a good turf, and until this was done, the new system could not be made to work. Old permanent grass was, if anything, even more difficult to convert to tillage. The land was often so rank that farmers could not stop the crops growing away from them, and it was frequently infested with leather-jackets and wireworms, which in due course would turn into crane-flies (daddy-long-legs) and click-beetles. These leather-jackets and wireworms lived by devouring the roots of corn and so destroying the crops. These pests could be got rid of only by stamping, rolling and crushing them to death, or by starving them out, either by long bare fallows or by planting a crop like woad that even they would not eat. All this took time and money. Thus to make a field of up-and-down land was a long job, and setting up an up-and-down farm took a matter of about a dozen years. During this time, too, the whole farm had to be cast into a new mould. Old grazing farms had to be split up now that the land was to be used so much more intensively; and several old common-field tenancies had to be knocked together to make a decent-sized farm. The common fields obviously needed to be enclosed, hedged and ditched, and the old grazing pastures subdivided into smaller closes. Then new outbuildings and farmhouses might have to be built, and new ponds made. Making an up-and-down farm was not a thing anyone could do. It took boldness, patience, and plenty of capital.

The leys of grass were kept down a long time, mostly six or seven years, and anything up to twelve. The period of tillage that followed varied greatly; it might be as short as two years or as long as five, but three or four was favoured by the best managers on middling soils. If the land had been enriched with marl, it could be ploughed for eight or nine years; and if it had first been planted with woad, for six or seven. Otherwise, seven would normally have been much too long, and those who tilled for nine, ten or even twelve were ploughing the heart out of the land. There were no hard and fast rules, however. Farmers tended to till one shift until another was ripe for ploughing up from grass and to graze one ley until the turf had formed on another.

When the leys were broken up it was usually in early spring. The turf was simply torn up and turned over, and oats or some other corn or pulse immediately sown. The next winter the field would be fallowed for barley or some other spring crop. As soon as this was harvested, the land was ploughed again, well mucked, and sown with wheat or rye. This last crop was intended to shelter and nurse a new sward of grass. There were thus about six ploughings in a dozen years and a crop of corn or grass every year.

Land was laid down simply by leaving the natural grasses to form a sward of themselves. The first essential in laying down, though it sounds Irish, was not to have ploughed the land out of heart beforehand. Then the field needed to be clean of weeds and left in raised but fairly broad and well-rounded ridges. The whole secret was that the fields, as George Barwell put it, had 'gotten some turf in 'em', and this turf had to be preserved through all the years of tillage. This was the great ulterior motive that led farmers to till for a limited number of years only, carefully to invert the turf when first ploughing up, and to fallow only in winter. The grass roots had to be kept alive all the time, so that a new ley of natural grass could arise from the ruins of the old one. In land that had been well manured and left in good heart, the grass soon came again.

These temporary leys were infinitely better than the permanent ones used by the old graziers and common-field farmers. Walter Blith did justice to them when he wrote,

'Do but look into and upon much of your new laid down land to graze, which being continually grazed doth put more proof into all sorts of goods, breed better, feed faster, milketh fruit-fuller than old pasture . . .; and in reason it must needs be so, because what grass comes fresh, is pure, without mixture, and sweet, being young and tender, and having no corrupt weeds or filth to annoy it, and fruitful, having heat and strength left in the land to feed it.'

Likewise temporary tillage was better than permanent. Fitz-herbert knew it would give 'plenty of corn with little dunging', and after the passage of a hundred years and more Blith had seen ample evidence of the fact that 'sometime ploughing one pasture and resting another' made 'fresh land and resty' that would 'bear more corn without manure than it did before with it'. In up-and-down husbandry, he justifiably says, 'one acre beareth the fruit of three, the two acres are preserved to graze'. This is really what happened: as much corn as before was obtained from one-third of the land, and the other two-thirds were put into grass that was a clear and absolute gain to the farmer.

In the common fields a ten-fold increase of harvest over seed was the most that the best cultivator could hope for. In up-and-down husbandry twenty-fold increases were common. Robert Herrick needed no poetic licence to write,

'Lord, 'tis thy plenty-dropping hand,
That soils my land,
And giv'st me, for my bushel sown,
Twice ten for one.'

To the same amount of corn harvested were now added great quantities of meat and milk, and all at a much lower cost per unit of produce, for the five ploughings within three years in the common fields were now replaced by five ploughings in ten years, and these on a smaller area of ploughland. Then if we additionally take account of the economies due to the increased scale of operations in the new, capital, up-and-down farms, it is easy to see how the new husbandry quartered unit costs, quadrupled output per acre, and produced great profits where none had existed before.

The new up-and-down farms were veritable cornucopias, pouring out a flood of beef, veal, mutton, lamb, cheese, butter, pork, bacon, eggs, barley, wheat, pulse, oats, wool, hides, skins, woad (*plate 8*), horses, poultry, flax, and hemp. Everything the common-field farmer could do, everything the mere grazier could do, the gentlemen and working farmers on up-and-down land could do better and cheaper. These farmers managed their stock much as the old graziers had done, except that the farmers bought in rather fewer cattle and bred more of their own, and also paid far more attention to dairy herds. But, above all, the new farmers stocked much more heavily than the old graziers had done, because they had much more grass nutrient from every acre. With more and better grass, farmers on up-and-down land succeeded in multiplying the production of meat, butter and cheese, and also of wool and hides, allowing the rapid development of the boot and shoe, hosiery, knitwear, and textile industries that gave whole or part-time employment to many of those who were unable or unwilling to partake of this new farming business.

This movement of labour power from agriculture to manufacturing industry is what was then, and since has been, denounced under the name of depopulation. Needless to say, there was no depopulation of the kingdom. Nor, so far as can be judged, was there any depopulation of the plain. Indeed, all the evidence points to a rapid upsurge of Midland population at this time. Nor, for that matter, does there appear to have been any depopulation of the countryside, for the industries that now grew and developed were mostly rural. What did certainly take place was a depopulation of agriculture, a 'putting down of ploughs', and a reduction of the agricultural work force. This inevitably accompanied the great economies made in plough-teams and cultivations. People in the past have tended either to denounce or deny such depopulation, which is absurd, for this economizing released hands for more productive work for the benefit of all, and not least of those made redundant in agriculture. Most people probably saw the wisdom of Joseph Lee's pointed remark, 'In vain that is done by more, which may be done by less'.

Similar types of up-and-down husbandry now began to play a larger part in the farming of the vales of Hereford, Berkeley, Evesham, Pickering, and London, of the Wealden Vales, of the Butter and Cheese Countries, and generally of all the plains and vales, as well as parts of the down, wold, heathland, and fen countries. The clearance of woodlands, especially in the Wealden Vales, and the greatly increased use of marl both here and in the Lancashire Plain and the Cheshire Cheese Country, created much more up-and-down land. From about 1590, too, the North-eastern Lowlands took to up-and-down husbandry instead of the previous shifting cultivation, and rapidly made up for lost time. Here this technical innovation was accompanied by other changes no less momentous. To an extent unequalled anywhere else, a mass of small peasant holdings was swept aside to make way for a restricted number of large capital farms that employed wage-labour and made great economies merely by virtue of their scale of operations. It could truthfully have been said of this clearance of estates that the turf huts of the petty tenants were profitably spread over the land, as manure. Finally, we must remember, the established up-and-down husbandries of the Woodland and High Suffolk continued as before. Small wonder, then, that one of the things that most impresses a Swedish observer in 1748 is that the 'English custom, for the most part, is, by turns, to lay down ploughed fields to meadows, and meadows to ploughed fields'. Up-and-down husbandry had triumphed.

Floating the Watermeadows

Next we come to the floating of watermeadows. There were two kinds of floating invented one after the other. Catchwork floating was brought in first, in the Vales of Hereford, and was designed for hill slopes. Ridge-and-furrow floating came later, in the Chalk Country, and was intended for flat river valleys. Both systems were essentially similar in that they resulted in a thin, one-inch sheet of water flowing over the meadow. Letting the water flow like this in summer could soon force a second crop of hay, but the greatest advantages were obtained by winter floating. It not only fertilized the meadow by dressing it with rich sediment; it also kept the land warm and safe from frosts and so allowed the grass to grow better and earlier. Hitherto, the month of April had been like an interregnum between the hay that had been stored for the winter and the new spring of grass. As the proverb said, 'While the grass grows, the horse starves'. This was a bottleneck farmers had always faced. It meant that their livestock often had short commons, and worse, that the number of animals the farmer could keep from one summer to the next was strictly limited to those which could be coaxed through this bleak period. Floating did away with this bottleneck, more, it made the neck wider than the bottle.

Previous efforts from about 1560 had made some progress in this direction, but real floating was invented by Rowland Vaughan of New Court and White House in the Golden Valley in or about 1589. He himself described his 'wetshod waterworks' in a lively and interesting little book. By a system of trenches, dams and sluices, the water was diverted from the main stream, taken along the contours of the hill just above the banks to be floated, and made to flow down the slope and all over the meadows by means of a descending array of gutters, before being drained away at the bottom (*figure 12*). When the streams were swollen by heavy rains and rich with sediments washed from ditches and fields, the floater opened his floodgates for a time and played the water over his meadow. Then, at the beginning of March, the gates were shut for the last time and the meadow was kept as dry 'as a child under the hands of a dainty nurse' and made ready for the sheep and cattle.

Vaughan's invention proved so profitable that the farmers and landowners roundabout made haste to imitate it. Before long the people of the Vales of Hereford had a new proverb: 'He that doth drown is a good husband'. By 1657 floating had become the accepted practice among the gentlemen farmers and cultivating squires who controlled most of the land, and had even

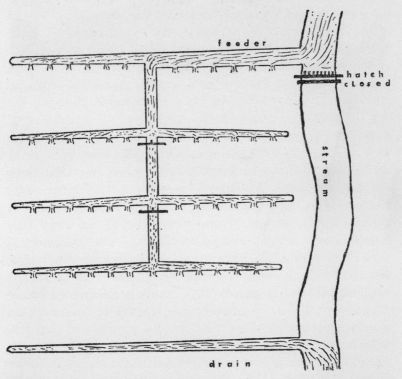

Fig. 12.   Plan of a catchwork floating meadow. The water runs down the slope from the feeder and returns to the stream via the drain.

been taken up by some of the relatively few common-field farmers. Not only old meadow and pasture were floated in this way; arable land was converted to rich meadow, raising its annual value eight- or ten-fold. The barrenest rabbit-warren could be made into meadow and many a man 'metamorphosed his wilderness' this way. Even old meadows newly floated became worth three times as much. More and better grass just at the time when it was most wanted meant that the farmers could rear greater numbers of improved Hereford cattle and keep larger flocks of Ryelands to enrich the arable.

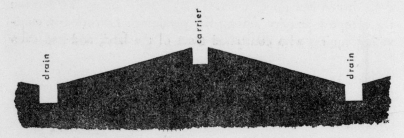

Fig. 13.   Profile of floating ridge and furrow. The water spills over from the carrier and is taken away by the drains.

By 1629 another method of floating had been invented that was suitable to the Chalk Country. In this ridge-and-furrow system, the water drawn off the river had to be passed along channels or carriers and branch-carriers set on elevated ridges and allowed to brim over and flow into corresponding drains or furrows. These ridges and furrows branched out until they formed a network over the whole 'pitch of work'. There was thus a 'regular disposition of water-carriages and drains, which, in a well laid-out meadow', we are told, would 'bring on and carry off the water as systematically as the arteries and veins do the blood in the human body' (*figures 13, 14, 15; plates 18, 19, 20, 21, 22*).

This form of floating was more difficult and expensive. Nevertheless, because of the closeness with which it could be fitted in with the sheep-and-corn husbandry of the Chalk Country, it brought commensurate rewards. For one thing, the

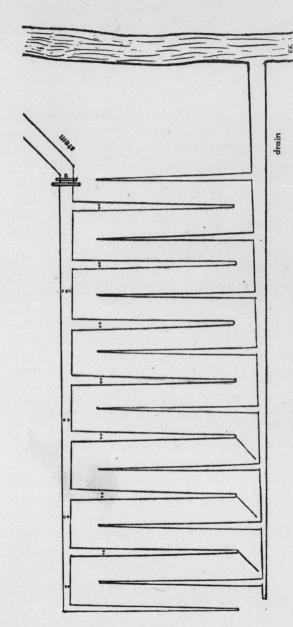

Fig. 14. Ridge-and-furrow floating on a regular surface. The plan shows the carriers leading off the stem, the drains leading to the main drain, the stops in the carriers to regulate the flow, and three tail-gutters. The water is not flowing.

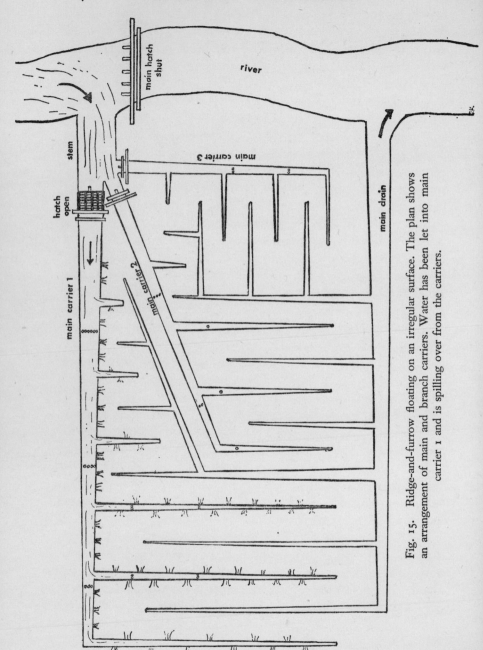

Fig. 15. Ridge-and-furrow floating on an irregular surface. The plan shows an arrangement of main and branch carriers. Water has been let into main carrier 1 and is spilling over from the carriers.

base of the meadows was so absorbent that a sheet of water could be kept running all through the winter months with only the rarest and shortest of breaks. Then, in times of heavy rain, the water-table rose so much and so quickly that the flood waters were so much the more turbulent and rich in sediment and dissolved chalk, all of which was deposited on the meadows. Thirdly, the floated meadows were used chiefly for the sheep, and especially for the ewes with their lambs, so that lambing could be made to coincide with the opening of the meadows about the middle of March, when their grass would be five or six inches high. Lastly, these same sheep were folded on the barley land at night. One day's feed of an acre of flowing meadow was plenty for the five hundred couples needed to fertilize an acre of arable. Only those who saw it could believe the value of a fold of couples of ewes and lambs coming immediately from a flowing meadow, with their bellies full of young, quick grass, and how much it could increase the quantity and improve the quality of a crop of barley. When in the watermeadows, the sheep were never suffered to lie down or to drop their dung and urine. All the manure was destined for the arable and as soon as they were seen to be full and disposed to lie down, the sheep were driven in haste to the tillage. Floating also enabled the farmers to fatten lambs and played a crucial part in increasing the size of Chalk Country sheep. Without the flowing meadow, the country could never have raised or supported so many sheep of so great a size.

The chief period of the construction of floated meadows in the Chalk Country was between 1629 and 1665. By 1716 floating had spread throughout the length and breadth of the country and was still gaining a little ground here and there.

By its very nature, floating belonged chiefly to the Vales of Hereford and the Chalk Country, and it could not spread everywhere. Nevertheless, it was taken up with varying degrees of success in some parts of the Chiltern and Poor Soils Countries and of the Midland Plain.

Draining the Fens

There was no great improvement to be wrought in the Fen
Country without first draining vast expanses into good winterground that could be cultivated throughout the year. It was this
tremendous task that was taken up in the last third of the
sixteenth century and more or less completed by 1653. As early
as 1589 it was realized that little betterment was to be hoped for
without 'straight cuts' or 'new rivers' to carry superfluous water
from the peat fens through enlarged outfalls to the sea. The
visible proof of this proposition was the increasing recourse
having to be made to pumping mills in the attempt to force
water to go where it would not flow of itself. As more and
more of the fenmoulds were drained in the early seventeenth
century by Captain Lovell and others, this need for new cuts
became ever more urgent and pressing, but people's minds
boggled at the enormous expense that would inevitably be
entailed. It was partly for this reason that the whole undertaking
was from the start bedevilled by strife between the 'slodgers'
and poor commoners of the one party, the local farmers and
landowners of the second, and those covetous kings James and
Charles I of the third.

On behalf of Charles, who took over his father's plans, an
Anglo-Dutch consortium of contractors headed by Cornelius
Vermuyden had some success in draining Hatfield Chase in
1626–7. By 1637, acting for a new joint-stock company set up
for the purpose by the Earl of Bedford and others, Vermuyden
had made the great mass of southern peat-fen into good summer-
ground, which much of it had never been before. The business
was then abruptly taken over by Charles and developed into a
project to make this land good winterground. By this means,
the king intended to make a killing for himself, at the expense
of the commoners and of the previous undertakers. But the
hostility he thus provoked from all the people of that country
grew into civil disturbances, in the course of which mobs defaced
and destroyed both these works, and others that were being
undertaken at the same time. When the civil war was over and

order restored, Vermuyden and the original company quickly made up for lost time and by 1652–3 had made the Bedford Level into good winterground. The great work was substantially completed (*plates 14, 15, 16*).

This draining turned out well for farmers. The fen soils were highly fertile, and only wanted to be given some body by a dressing of clay or marl. Indeed, they had so much humus that some of it had to be got rid of by paring the turf and burning it away. The climate, too, greatly favoured the cultivation of crops. A special form of up-and-down husbandry was adopted. The chief cereal grown was oats, but this crop was usually preceded by one of hemp, flax, woad, mustard, or, most frequently, of cole-seed (*plate 7*). This rape or cole-seed had long been grown in the Marshland and other well-drained areas, but now it spread and multiplied over the whole country. The seed was sown at intervals from May onwards so as to produce a succession of crops for folding off to sheep in autumn and winter. It was a splendid crop for fattening sheep and gave more green food an acre than turnips could have done. And when the sheep had finished with it, provided the spring was reasonably mild, the plant continued to flourish, and could then be reaped like corn in the summer and its seeds threshed out and sold to the mills for crushing for oil.

Confounding all the gloomy prophets, improved drainage still left the farmers plenty of feed and fodder. Temporary grass, and the saltings, gave plenty of summer feed, and cole-seed made green feed in winter that more than made up for the loss of coarse fen-fodder. Farmers could now fatten sheep both in summer and in winter, when they fetched the best prices, especially at first when this was the only winter mutton available. More sheep were kept and fattened, and still there was enough grass to boost the output of beef and maintain the production of cheese and butter, as well as of pig-meat and veal. Brood mares went on being used for draught purposes, and whereas the peat-fens had formerly been unable to bear the weight of any but ponies, they could now support heavy shire horses, which could thus be bred in much greater numbers.

Farming of this kind could only be carried on by wealthy capital farmers. The 'slodgers' and petty family or part-time farmers who had formerly inhabited the fens were now replaced by at least as many working farmers, each of whom employed several wage-labourers about his business. There was thus no question of there being any depopulation. On the contrary, the land now became properly peopled for the first time.

Drainage not altogether unlike that in the Fen Country was attempted in the Western Waterlands, especially in King's Sedgemoor, but with far less success and with less hope of profit, for this was best suited to remain predominantly a grassland country. In the Lancashire Plain and the Cheshire Cheese Country the mosses or fens, though numerous, were mostly far less extensive, and the draining of them was so much the easier and cheaper. All that was really needed was a system of sod-drains and then either paring and burning or marling, and there was plenty of slippery, fat marl to be found not far underground. This period, too, saw a great upsurge in the reclamation of land from the sea in the Lancashire Plain, the Fen, Saltings and Sand-lings Countries, the Norfolk Heathlands, the vales of Berkeley and London, and even in Romney Marsh itself.

Root Crops

Carrots, parsnips and turnips, along with cabbages, onions, and many other vegetables, had long been grown in kitchen and market gardens, and were, accordingly, eating varieties and intended for the table. In those days market-gardening depended on big supplies of stable manure from large towns, and on rotating or alternating vegetable and corn crops, the whole business being conducted along the lines of the horti-cum-agriculture practised by the Flemish peasants, who were regarded as market-gardeners by the people of England when they migrated here from Flanders, since the plough was used only in preparation for the spade. Turnips, in particular, were a favourite table vegetable and much cultivated not only in kitchen and market-gardens of the usual sort but also in hemp gardens after the hemp and in hop-gardens under the hops. The great invention now made in England was the field cultivation by farmers of new varieties of some of these root and other crops for the purpose of feeding livestock.

The first crop to be adopted in this way was the carrot, which was introduced and established in the Sandlings Country in the period 1590–1610. This country was extraordinarily favourable to carrots, for in its deep sandy soils they could apple out well and push their roots down to the subsoil. The fields were winter-fallowed and seeds harrowed in about the end of March. During growth the carrots were hoed, to a depth of about seven inches, two or three times. They were then left to stand in the field, all winter if necessary, and pulled when required. Some of the surplus was exported to London for the stables, but the greater part of the crop provendered horses in the Sandlings Country itself, releasing hay and oat-straw for the sheep and cattle. The punches' usual diet became eighty bushels of carrots a week to a stable of six; together with as much as they wanted of chaff, which was made up of two parts straw to one of hay; rarely any oats, and corn of any sort only when they were to be put to extraordinary exertions. On this fare they worked strongly from six in the morning until six at night, with a midday break of two and a half hours; and under this management Suffolk punches became the best breed of special farm horse in the kingdom and famous for their never-say-die attitude to the heaviest work. About 1670–90 the Vale of Taunton Deane took up carrot cultivation on a great scale. In all but the extreme south, the vale consisted largely of natural carrot soils and here both the cultivation and the utilization of the crop were much like those in the Sandlings Country. By 1618 the farmers near Bury St Edmunds in the Breckland were growing carrots, and by the early eighteenth century those occupying the few sandy soils in the Chalk Country and the Midland Plain were doing likewise. Farmers generally could not follow suit, for deep, sandy, carrot soils were to be found in few other places and in none where carrot-growing could be fitted into the general plan of farm management.

Then, between the years 1646 and 1656 the High Suffolk

farmers suddenly took to growing turnips. Land that was destined to be fallowed in any event was ploughed up as soon as the corn had been harvested and turnips were then sown after a single ploughing and mucking. It had been usual to fallow for one year during each succession of tillage crops and this fallow was now largely sown to turnips instead of to buckwheat or instead of being left bare. In this way, buckwheat or worse was exchanged for turnips and the fallows were retained, for what with ploughing, singling, and frequent hand-hoeing, the land was as well fallowed as it ever had been. In autumn the first roots were ready to be eaten and some were drawn and stored in the turnip shed for immediate use, while the remainder were left in the ground to be lifted as and when required. Being hard varieties, these turnips were suitable for pulling and could safely be left in the ground all through the winter. From their shed the turnips were taken, together with the traditional hay and straw, to the milking cows in their yards or houses, so that milking continued uninterruptedly throughout the year, the last of the roots not being pulled until the field was prepared for barley about March. In addition, some bullocks were fattened on turnips during the winter.

Turnip cultivation then spread in about 1666–71, to East Norfolk; and the farmers here borrowed from High Suffolk the sideline of fattening bullocks on turnips for winter beef. Then, during 1673–7, this same practice spread from East Norfolk and High Suffolk to the Norfolk Heathlands and the Sandlings Country. However, as these were primarily sheep-and-corn countries the farmers could not make so much use of the hard varieties of turnips as the cow countries did, and instead also took to growing the white varieties that could be fed off in the fields to folding flocks in order to produce winter mutton and lamb and still further to enrich the land for corn. This new system was probably invented first in the Chiltern Country and was certainly adopted by the farmers there in, and immediately after 1673, and thence was introduced, about 1675–84, to the Norfolk Heathlands (save for the extreme north of this region, where the innovation was delayed until the second or even the third quarter of the eighteenth century). In the period 1675–99 it was introduced in the Northdown, Chalk and Oxford Heights countries, and to some extent in the Breckland; and about 1684–99 in the Sandlings Country. These twin innovations, having been generally diffused throughout several countries, were now taken up by all hands in all suitable places. Turnips were grown in the drained fens of the Fen, Saltings and Cheshire Cheese Countries and in the pockets of free-draining loams in the Midland Plain and the Vale of Evesham. In the opening years of the eighteenth century they were adopted in the Cotswold and Northwold Countries, in the North-eastern Lowlands, in the Sherwood district of the Peak-Forest Country, and here and there even in the rarely propitious Woodland and the West Country. By 1756 field turnips had even reached the North-western Lowlands.

It goes without saying that turnip cultivation was no more universally applicable in those days than hydro-electric schemes are today. After all, God made the world and poor man makes the best he can of it. Many places and virtually whole countries in England were entirely lacking in turnip soils, even if turnips could have been fitted into their husbandries. Many soils were either too shallow or too wet and heavy for any variety of turnip to apple out in, and in sticky and retentive land hard turnips could not be pulled nor white ones fed off without poaching the fields and spoiling them for crops, and rotting any sheep put into them.

In such soils, dwarf rape provided a useful substitute for turnips, and this crop had made its appearance in the Midland Plain by 1686. Here and in the Vale of Pickering and the Chalk Country, rape eventually became hardly less important than turnips elsewhere. Cabbages served as well, or better, in deep and heavy soils, and having been first invented at Wimborne St Giles, in the Poor Soils Country, about 1660–70, were taken up in some Midland farms, and in High Suffolk, where to some extent they replaced turnips, especially when the fly was on the turnip. Moreover, the potato graduated from the kitchen garden and became the characteristic crop and show-piece of cultivation in the drained mosslands of the Lancashire Plain in the years immediately preceding 1690. Before long the farmers with moss-land in the Cheshire Cheese Country followed this example, and later those in the Fen Country; but nowhere was this humble tuber so important to the farmers as in the Lancashire Plain, where it was grown mainly as a succulent fodder for young cattle. It was unsuitable for dairy cows or for fattening stock. And not until a later age, when corn became scarce, would English people accept potatoes day in and day out both in and out of season.

Among the other new crops introduced at this time were weld and tobacco. The growing of English tobacco (*plate 10*) was already well established in the Vale of Evesham by 1619, and by 1627 in or near Wootton Bassett, in the Oxford Heights Country. Weld (dyer's weed) was first cultivated about 1610 in the North-down Country, especially in the valley of the Great Stour, and not long after was being grown also at Narford and elsewhere in the Norfolk Heathlands, and in the Chiltern Country. It was usually sown under oats or barley, fed off by sheep in the first year, and cropped in the second for the sake of its yellow dyestuff.

In the sheep-and-corn countries, the same thin and all too easily exhausted soil that so suited sheep also gave a splendid opportunity for getting more fodder and forage by growing fields of sainfoin, which thrust down its tap-root and fed in the subsoil rather than the soil and then gave one rich mow of hay every year for five years, not to speak of the useful aftermaths. Since its stonebrash soils were so easily exhausted and its meadows could not be floated, the Cotswold Country was the one that stood in the greatest need of sainfoin and was the first to introduce the crop in or about 1650. Hardly more than a year passed before the Chiltern and Northdown Countries started on the same course. From its base in the Cotswold Country sainfoin spread like wildfire to the Oxford Heights and Chalk Countries, and to the Norfolk Heathlands. From its base in the Chiltern Country the new crop moved into the Breckland, and from there it probably made a second point of entry into the Norfolk

Heathlands. Before long, too, it was taken up in the Northwold Country. In all these countries, by 1675, sainfoin had become a crop as ordinary as any other. In addition, sainfoin found its way swiftly and unerringly into the few suitable places in the Midland Plain, and eventually to those in the West Country. Lucerne, another lover of chalky and limy land, was introduced in the Northdown Country. Elsewhere, however, it was hardly found except in suburban hay-farms or hobby farms, largely because the climate would not allow it to produce seeds that would germinate.

Clover cultivation was not in itself anything new in the second half of the seventeenth century, for 'claver-grass', 'honeysuckle-grass' and almost all types of clover, had been sown along with other hayseeds for ages, and for at least half a century had been selected and added to hayseeds for the purpose of making both permanent and temporary leys. What was new in the latter half of the seventeenth century was the selection of seeds of particular varieties of clover for sowing by themselves, as an always less costly and often more productive alternative to tares and vetches for hay and forage; or as a measured proportion of a specially prepared mixture of clover and grass 'seeds' for mainly temporary leys. The clovers, of course, shared with peas, beans, tares and vetches, lentils and other leguminous crops, the virtue of being able to 'fix' nitrogen in the soil and so produce nitrogenous compounds that served as plant food. Similarly, rye-grass had likewise been cultivated for ages, but only now began to be specially selected, along with certain other kinds of grass. The first country to invent the cultivation of selected clovers and 'seeds' and of separate clover crops was the Wealden Vales. These innovations started here in 1649 and had run their course by 1669. The same twin innovations were carried out in the Midland Plain between 1660 (or slightly before) and 1675. In the Vales of Hereford, while selected clovers arrived on the scene shortly after 1650, 'seeds' mixtures were not fully adopted until almost 1690. In the West Country the innovations took much the same chronological course, but in the Vale of Taunton Deane they were commenced in the early 1660s and completed by or just after 1670. East Norfolk also saw the triumph of clover and 'seeds' between 1664 and 1671. High Suffolk started at much the same time, but arrived at completion as late as 1675, or perhaps even 1684. Except in its northern district, where the innovations dragged on until about 1690, they were finished in the Norfolk Heathlands by 1674. Although the Northdown and Chiltern Countries were among the earliest to take up clover research and development, selected clover and 'seeds' were not in general use in the former until about 1670, and in the latter not perhaps until 1675. In the Saltings Country 1679 seems to have been the terminal date for these twin innovations, and it was in the last quarter of the century that they established themselves in the Oxford Heights, Chalk, Petworth, Southdown, Fen, South Seacoast, and, probably, the Sandlings Countries, in the Vale of Evesham and in certain favoured parts of the Breckland and the Blackheath Countries. At much the same time, the Woodland, the Cheshire Cheese Country and the Vale of Berkeley adopted the new inventions to the limited extent to which they were applicable and acceptable. In some countries, however, the time lag was greater, and the Cotswold, Northwold and Poor Soils Countries, Wales and the North-eastern Lowlands caught up with the others only in the opening years of the eighteenth century, and the Vale of Pickering (where they were not much help) and the North-western Lowlands (last as usual) not until the middle of the century. In short, these innovations were commenced just after 1650, boomed from 1661, reached their peak in about 1670 and then slowly receded. By and large, England was 'in clover' by 1718, for in that year the countries that had not adopted the innovations were mostly those dairy-grazing ones where clover would have spoiled the cheese and butter and where natural herbage generally gave more suitable milk.

It was largely better manuring that allowed clover cultivation to spread as far and fast as it did, and much of this manure arose from the heavier stocking that the new crops and other improvements allowed. But much also came from extraneous fertilizers. Where obtainable and applicable, marls were in more or less

continual use, but after about 1560 farmers marled far more than
before, especially in the Wealden Vales, the Lancashire Plain and
the Cheshire Cheese Country, where they were able by this
means greatly to extend the acreage of up-and-down land. By
the early seventeenth century marls were being dug from five
or more fathoms and marl beds prospected with the augers that
had been developed for deep mining. Marl was also used heavily
in the Oxford Heights Country, the Norfolk Heathlands and
elsewhere. And then at the end of the sixteenth century and the
early part of the seventeenth, as the land became gradually
sated with marl, its place was taken by heavy dressings of lime.
Thanks largely to the lowering of its cost by burning it with
coal fuel, lime came into increasingly widespread and heavy use
from about 1560 onwards. The Vale of Pickering, the Butter,
Cheese and Cheshire Cheese Countries, and the Lancashire and
Midland Plains were among the foremost users of lime, but lime
and chalk were set to work transforming the arable lands of
country after country. It was the rise of the coal industry more
than any other industrial event that enriched the farm lands of
England. Thanks to coal, lime became cheap. Thanks to coal,
farmers stopped burning cow-pats and put them on the land
instead. Thanks to coal, farmers no longer looked to the fens,
mosses and moors for peat-fuel and thought rather to drain them
off ready for the plough. Every advance in the extractive, processing and manufacturing industries, however, tended towards
the production of more and better fertilizers for the farms. Sea-
coal ash, soot, urry, soap-ash, waste brine, tanner's muck, saw,
malt and coal-dust, rags, clippings of fur, shavings of horn,
shreds of leather, and all manner of industrial refuse was returned
to the land. And in Wales, the West Country and elsewhere,
sea-sand or ooze, and seaweed were ploughed into the arable far
more than in previous times.

With all these rich new sources of fodder and forage being
exploited by the farmers, it is hardly surprising that the first and
chief beneficiaries were the farm animals themselves. The drainage
of the fens enabled a far greater number of shire horses to be
bred, and the introduction of carrots in the Sandlings Country

and the Vale of Taunton Deane, coupled with clover and 'seeds', allowed more and better punches and other horses to be reared. Catchwork floating benefited especially the Hereford breed of cattle, and potatoes the longhorns, but all gained in size and numbers from up-and-down husbandry, from extra marling and liming, and from the new crops. The spread of up-and-down husbandry, and then speeding up of grassing over by the selection of clovers and seeds, in the Midland Plain, North-eastern Lowlands and elsewhere meant that increasing numbers of pasture sheep displaced the dwindling flocks of fallow ones. Fed on sainfoin, rye-grass, clovers and turnips, and crossed with the Midland pasture breed, the Cotswold sheep were entirely transformed. Their legs became shorter, their carcasses larger and fleshier and their fleeces suited to worsted rather than to woollens. As a result especially of floating, the Chalk Country sheep grew larger (for some farmers, too large) in stature, longer in the leg and higher and heavier in the fore-quarters, while, thanks to clover and other superior feed, their fleeces deteriorated. Much the same happened to the Ryeland wool, especially when their pastures were limed and enriched with selected clover and 'seeds'. Better feed, too, caused the East Anglian sheep to grow in weight and size and produce more twins and triplets. Partly by grazing on the new crops and partly by being crossed with the already improved Fen breed, the Northwold sheep gave birth to a new race yielding more meat and a heavier fleece of mainly worsted quality. In other ways, too, scientific breeding was married to the new crops to improve or change livestock strains. Already by 1560 selective breeding was being employed to improve the Midland pasture sheep by crossing them with those of the Fen and Saltings Countries. In the early eighteenth century famous Midland stock-breeders like Hartopp and Tate were buying Fen rams that had been forced to a great size on cole-seed. Then, from the improved pasture sheep that resulted, the Midland breeders Stone and Allom, by a combination of superior feeding and breeding in-and-in, produced the New Leicester pasture sheep later perfected at Dishley by Robert Bakewell, who likewise combined inbreeding with high feeding on cabbages, rape, clover and 'seeds' and floating grasses. Selected breeding and better feed similarly gave rise to the superior strain of Teeswater cattle known as Durham shorthorns, which stemmed from a bull sired in 1737. The longhorns were made better by the breeding and feeding methods employed by Tate and other Midland breeders at the turn of the seventeenth and eighteenth centuries. Tate's cattle were still further improved by the same means by Webster of Canley in about 1750, and from the Canley herd, Princip, Bakewell and Fowler drew their stock when they tried to develop a new specialist beef breed. This unfortunately proved a bad speculation, as most farmers continued to prefer dual-purpose breeds.

Although faster at some times than others, the progress of up-and-down husbandry was more or less continuous throughout the age of the agricultural revolution. It was this invention, too, that gave the greatest opportunities to men of enterprise. Moreover, it absorbed a larger total of capital than any other single improvement. The creation of up-and-down farms was the work of years, not months; and the capital required for conversion and reconstruction, for building, hedging and ditching, pond-making, and for the legal expenses involved in division, allotment and enclosure, was tied up for a long time before it could show any return. The same was true to a rather lesser degree in the floating of watermeadows. This improvement took months rather than weeks, and many farmers invested scores of pounds, and some many hundreds, in it. Thousands of pounds were sunk in drainage schemes in different countries, and the Fen Country, in particular, attracted large investments from land-owners and financiers. Marling, too, was a relatively expensive improvement. In contrast to these, most new crops could be adopted rapidly, easily, and cheaply. Sainfoin, potatoes, carrots and turnips were all like this. Cole-seed cultivation was rather more expensive to start up, because it entailed paring and burning and marling. It seems to have taken a good deal to perfect the growing of selected clovers. Clover-sickness, which was brought on by trying to repeat the crop too frequently, was an unexpected snag, and one that was overcome only after a good deal of trial

and error. Nevertheless even the most expensive introduction
of a new crop was cheaper than the works involved in making
up-and-down farms, floating watermeadows, and draining fens.
Since it was in the hundred years after 1560 that these three
great works were mostly undertaken, it may be inferred that this
period saw also the bulk of the investment needed for the agricultural revolution.

It will be observed, too, that the countries where the most
expensive and far-reaching innovations were made were the
ones where large-scale capitalist farming was introduced simul-
taneously and for the first time. The two extremes that best
illustrate this point are the Woodland and the North-eastern
Lowlands. No country experienced more dramatic technical
changes than the latter, and it was here that there took place
the most abrupt and thoroughgoing supplanting of a mass of
poverty-stricken peasants by a set of wealthy farmers. The
Woodland, however, was already in the hands of gentlemen and
working farmers in the early sixteenth century, and here agricultural improvement had already been taken almost as far as it
could go. It was not the countries with the greatest existing
concentration of farming capital that saw the greatest innovations,
but the countries with the greatest scope for innovations that
attracted new concentrations of capital.

The innovations in agriculture set the tone and beat the
tempo of business life in the countryside and, indirectly, elsewhere also. The period between 1560–85 was one of booming
agricultural prosperity thanks largely to the innovation of up-and-
down husbandry. A minor recession only prepared the way for
a new and powerful upsurge that was not played out until about
1615: carrot cultivation and catchwork floating were introduced;
drainage and cole-seed growing got into their stride; and up-and-
down husbandry expanded in the Midland Plain, was taken up
elsewhere, and suddenly invaded the North-eastern Lowlands.
Tobacco and weld cultivation was also begun. 1620 and thereabouts was clearly a time of difficulty and depression, due to an
avalanche of farm goods glutting the markets and forcing down
prices; farm rents, and corn, dairy-produce, meat, cattle and wool

prices all took a tumble. 'We are here in a strange case to complain of plenty', reported Chamberlain, the well-known letter-writer of the period. But the fruit of invention and competition was not yet fully formed. A fresh flood of innovations restored buoyancy to the markets. Up-and-down husbandry, catchwork floating, and fen drainage and cultivation went from strength to strength, and ridge-and-furrow floating started in the Chalk Country. Then the rest of the new crops were invented one after the other in quick succession. When all this had been done, nothing could hinder prices from first collapsing and then languishing. Once again, there appeared the 'strange paradox, that plenty should make the Kingdom poor'. Landlords complained that clover had ruined rents from meadowlands and many of them took a distinct dislike to all improvements. William Petty was far from being the only man to realize that these low prices had been caused by the great expansion of production that had taken place thanks to fen drainage, floating, sainfoin, clover and other innovations. Temporary-grass beef, cole-seed mutton, turnip butter, and cheap wheat and barley now flooded on to the markets. However, it is an ill wind that blows no good. When prices fell, we can readily understand how 'All farmers generally murmured at this plenty and cheapness' and why landowners should say, 'Plenty hath made us poor'. But consumers welcomed the low prices with open arms.

Chapter Five

AN OPULENT PEOPLE

The English Improvers

The improvers were either the originators of new farming processes and products or their early imitators, and in the present state of knowledge it is hardly possible to distinguish the former from the latter. Agricultural innovators were seldom chronicled and even more rarely renowned. Their very memory was usually lost within three generations. For this reason, it was usual in those days to discuss these matters in terms of improvements and improvers. This made good sense, for hardly anyone knew who the inventor was, and it did not really matter very much, for any successful innovation would immediately be taken up by rapidly widening circles of imitators, all of whom helped to bring in the new invention.

These agricultural improvers were drawn from all ranks of rural society. Some of them, indeed, were wealthy men to start off with; but the others wound up wealthy; and we usually have difficulty in telling one lot from the other. It was because he 'worked miracles by turning stones into bread', or by making two blades of grass grow where only one grew before, that the improver had 'a great estate raised out of nothing', and we frequently only run across him in the records when he was already a made man or had been on the make for some time.

We must count ourselves fortunate, then, for any stray items of information that come our way. Rowland Vaughan, the inventor of catchwork floating was a landed gentleman in the Vales of Hereford, but only in his wife's right. He had married into the estate, and but for this would never, in all probability, have enjoyed those idle moments in those meadows which gave rise to the invention. His great brainwave came when he was at a loose end and thinking about nothing in particular. (Most discoveries, of course, are made by accident, when shaving or gazing into the fire, or some such, and not on purpose.) The Nicholas Hall who removed from Dundry Hill to North Wraxall and there became the inventor of sainfoin cultivation ended up as a gentleman farmer, but we know little of his earlier life. Sir Richard Weston, who was much concerned with research and development for clover and other new crops, was a middling landowner. Sir William Ashley, who pioneered cabbage-growing, was of similar standing. But the other inventors are as yet unknown.

The great inventions were made by a small handful of men of genuinely creative ability, but a crowd of imitators pressed at their heels. They waited at first to see how the innovations turned out. Some must have failed, and on that account have been consigned to oblivion, but many succeeded and proved themselves in practice. William Folkingham voiced the thoughts of the ordinary man when he said, 'We are too wise, holding it ridiculous to innovate, nay to imitate anything not approved by continual practice'. But once an innovation had proved itself profitable, everyone wanted to take it up. When Nicholas Hall started cultivating sainfoin, 'It turned to great profit to him, which hath made his neighbours to imitate him'. Lord Scudamore and others of his neighbours lost no time in following Vaughan's example in the matter of floating. This was the way innovations spread. They were taken up rapidly because they were open for all to see. No agricultural invention was patented, for the simple reason that it could only be made in the sight of the whole world and could not possibly be kept secret from anyone. To learn new techniques one had only to lean over the gate and gaze. Emulation was easy.

The diffusion of innovations was also assisted by certain technical services provided by specialists. Itinerant woadmen would undertake to plough up an old pasture and show the proprietor how to make the best of it. Seedsmen and their agents were only too anxious to assist farmers in trying out new crops. And there was a growing profession of civil engineers to aid in or take charge of the works required for some improvements. Such a gentleman was John Knight of Stockton, who was the first floating engineer that we know of.

It was the gentlemen farmers and cultivating squires who were busiest in taking up and diffusing new techniques once they were proven. Men of this kind hastened to copy Rowland Vaughan's work. When John Aubrey discusses the spread of ridge-and-furrow floating in his neighbourhood he mentions only well-to-do gentlemen like John Bayly of Bishop's Down. All the Chalk Country men who played a leading or active part in floating the watermeadows were wealthy farmers. It was Sir John Turner who spread sainfoin cultivation from the Cotswold Country to parts of the Norfolk Heathlands. In all the livestock improvements made in the Midland Plain, it was gentlemen farmers and cultivating squires who were concerned. John Spencer, who founded the famous ram-breeding flock at Wormleighton early in the sixteenth century, and Robert Bakewell, whose family had farmed and ploughed Dishley Grange Farm for some generations, were typical of these gentlemen stockbreeders. The first turnip growers we meet are in High Suffolk and East Norfolk, substantial working or gentlemen farmers, and in the Norfolk Heathlands cultivating landowners like the Walpoles and the Townshends.

The little common-field farmers also imitated the new inventions, but only tardily and reluctantly. They were willing to let everyone else have a go at it before they did. Clover was grown in Maddingley common fields as early as 1662, sainfoin in those of Hitchin by 1685, and rape in those of Clayworth by 1688; but these were exceptional cases. The great mass of common-field farmers only adopted clover and 'seeds' in the Midland Plain in the period 1694–1739; in the Cotswold Country, along with sainfoin, only in 1690–1748; in the Vale of Evesham from 1704 or a little earlier; and in the Chalk Country in 1716–23. Turnips they only took to in 1723–40, 1743–56, 1724–30, and about 1740 respectively. Common-field farmers joined with others under the leadership of the capital farmers to float watermeadows, but willy-nilly rather than of their own volition. It usually happened that the demesne farmer was only able to float his own meadows if he could come to some arrangement with the petty tenantry for sharing and controlling the waters of the stream, and then he had often to pay a high price for their consent. We find, for instance, a cottager who stubbornly refused to let the farmer float the demesne meadows at all unless and until he floated the cottager's meadow for him gratis and allowed him to put ten sheep in the demesne pastures as well.

Second only to the wealthy farmers in taking up and bringing in the new improvements were the landowners. Many ran their own home farms and often first introduced the innovations on their own land and then encouraged their tenant farmers to follow suit. The Walpoles, for example, grew turnips themselves and persuaded their farmers to do likewise. Even when they were above engaging in cultivation themselves, enlightened landowners were anxious, in their own interests, to encourage or assist their tenants to undertake improvements. Thus we find the Earl of Pembroke's steward presiding over a meeting of the farmers of Wylye when they decided to co-operate in floating their meadows. Lord Hastings was present in the manor court when the Puddletown farmers debated and agreed to a similar project. The Earl of Bedford was only the most famous and venturesome of the many landowners who undertook or organized the drainage of fens and marshes. It was the enlightened landed gentry, too, who took the leading part in organizing enclosures by agreement, by which means common fields and lands were divided, allotted and enclosed, while preserving and maintaining all the property rights of all the proprietors of all interests and estates in the land, and at the same time making generous provision for the less fortunate who had no such property.

Successful improvers reaped great profits, just as unsuccessful ones faced disastrous losses. Robert Bakewell soon found himself in queer street when his strain of longhorn cattle proved unacceptable to farmers. But this failure has only been recorded because Bakewell had already made himself famous by his successful ventures. Most failures are soon forgotten. Success is what resounds, and there were successes in plenty. Even in the absence of any considerable technical improvement, when from a demesne let out to service-tenants was created a capital farm worked by wage-labour, the rewards were substantial. Robert Loder, who succeeded in doing this, raised his return from some £150 a year to £200. A little later another Chalk Country farmer was making between £145 and £180 a year. A modest Midland farmer, in his first few years in business netted about £100 a year. In addition, profits could be boosted by technical innovations. Ploughing up a ley could give several pounds profit an acre on the corn alone. Turnips gave about £1 an acre profit and cole-seed about £2. An enterprising farmer could make anything up to £100 a year from turnips alone, £500 on corn from grass, and £1,000 on cole-seed. The profits of floating were enormous. In point of fact, farmers seldom bothered to calculate their profits from such innovations; they were content to enjoy the small fortunes they had made; but we can see enough to know that enterprise was handsomely rewarded. Old meads newly floated often trebled their value. When floating converted arable to rich meadowland annual values rose six-, eight- or ten-fold. Vaughan increased the value of his demesne lands seven- or eight-fold, and this was nothing out of the way for the Vales of Hereford. In the Chalk Country, floating multiplied rental values between three- and sixty-fold. By marling their land, enterprising farmers and landowners in the Lancashire Plain, the Cheshire Cheese Country, the Wealden Vales, and elsewhere, were able to double its value. When summerground was converted to winterground in the Fen Country, the whole basis of farm valuation was changed. The fen, which no one previously ever bothered to value separately, now became worth far more than all the rest of the farm put together.

The expectation of private profit thus lured men to strive for the welfare of all. Investment in improvements increased production and the capacity to produce. The improvers baked a much larger cake for others to share. Up-and-down husbandry increased net yields more than four-fold. Floating raised the output of grass and hay about five-fold and boosted corn yields into the bargain. The new crops swelled the herds and flocks and heaped up the granaries. Private profit signalled the common benefit.

The improvers made the agricultural revolution; but what caused them to act so? What caused this agricultural revolution? The answer to this question, which might formerly have seemed exceedingly difficult, has been made apparent by what has already been said. Improvement of this kind is what creative and able people will set their hands to in the ordinary course of things, provided only that rights of private property are assured and they have sound money with which to carry on their trade. Nothing short of the general insecurity of private property or the inflation of currency by the state can stop men from bettering themselves. By 1560 sound money had been restored after the debasements of the first half of the century, so there was no trouble on this score. As for private property, it had long been secure in general, but what was here of particular and crucial significance was the security of the property that farmers had in their interest or estate in the land through the leases that they took. Here again, all was well. Most leasehold property had long enjoyed legal security, and the last loophole in the laws that assured farmers their property was effectively closed in 1499. Ever since then every English farmer, no matter how humble, has been 'lord paramount within himself, though he hold by never so mean a tenure'.

The rule of law, sanctity of private property, and sound currency gave complete liberty to each individual to follow his natural inclinations in improving his own lot. Under these circumstances innovators were able to use their native wit and inventiveness in seeking their own profit, and other improvers were able to imitate and spread the innovations that proved profitable. This leaves only the question, why were these particular inventions and improvements made? The answer is, these were the ones that most successfully satisfied the correctly anticipated demands of consumers, and therefore showed the greatest profit. Those men who speculated that consumers in future would demand more meat, butter, and cheese proved right; and those who reorganized production to meet these expected demands had profits to show as the visible proof of their success. As to the causes of the nature of consumers' demands, it hardly needs to be demonstrated that those who already have plenty of bread will want meat, butter and cheese to eat with it.

In short, the real cause of the agricultural revolution is that the improvers were given a chance. Human nature saw to the rest.

A New Way to Get Wealth

Improvement was the new way to wealth. Even in the capital-farm countries there always remained a gradation of farms from small to large. The merging of many small farms into fewer large ones in some countries only extended the ladder upwards and broadened it out at the top. It became a bit narrower at the bottom, but this did not matter, for it was still left wide enough for all who could climb. And small farms were no less numerous than they had always been, for as fast as they were swept away in the capital-farm countries, new ones were made in the dairy-grazing ones, especially as the royal forests were cleared and occupied. Farming was still a career open to all the talents and now there were far more good openings. On their way up the scale, men moved from farm to farm until they reached the pinnacle of their achievement. This meant there were at least as many standards of living among them as there were rungs in the ladder, and just as each rung was but a step in life, so each standard was merely a passing phase. Those at the bottom were poorer (a purely relative adjective), because they had not yet got their feet off the first rung. Cottagers were seldom well-off, because when they were they got themselves little farms and stopped being cottagers. Family farmers who did well branched out into grazing or took larger farms and hired labour to work them. A working farmer who made money would start to set himself up as a gentleman. And a rich gentleman farmer would eventually secure his wealth by buying land, so that he could retire on rents.

The improvers profited from their improvements and those who climbed to the top of the farming ladder improved their standards of life. Feather beds, carpets and tapestries all came into general use among capital farmers. Their pewter grew more abundant and silver and sometimes gold plate adorned their houses, while treen or wooden platters and spoons went out of fashion. One of the marks of the age was this 'exchange of vessel, as of treen platters into pewter, and wooden spoons into silver or tin'. A farmer who was anything of a success would now, as William Harrison tells us,

'think his gains very small towards the end of his term if he have not six or seven years' rent lying by him, therewith to purchase a new lease, beside a fair garnish of pewter on his cupboard, with so much more in odd vessel going about his house, three or four feather beds, so many coverlets and carpets of tapestry, a silver salt, a bowl for wine (if not a whole nest), and a dozen of spoons to furnish up the suit.'

An ordinary working farmer might have tin buttons on his weekday suit, but silver buttons on his Sunday one, and silver plate might shine on his dresser.

Most gentlemen and working farmers came to reside in manor houses and other capital messuages best described as fit for a lord, with, say, two storeys, each of a dozen rooms, or three or four smaller storeys, built at the least of timber, plaster and thatch, and more and more frequently of brick and tiles or stone and slate, and with glazed windows. Old farmhouses were energetically extended and modernized, new storeys and wings added, and great chimney stacks built on (*figure 16*).

Perhaps the clearest hallmark of good living among these farmers, however, and what singled them out from their lesser brethren, was the acquisition of gentility itself. By no means all who were gentlemen in nature were such in name also. Some farmers were content to go on being styled yeomen long after they had taken to joining in field sports with the lesser gentry and had come to be regarded as suitable matches for gentle-women. What did it matter if one's friends and neighbours still called one Goodman, or Goodie for short, as long as one had a pack of beagles and coursed hares with Master This and Master That? 'His outside is an ancient yeoman of England, though his

Fig. 16. East Overton Farmhouse 1567. A contemporary drawing of the demesne farmer's house in a Chalk-Country township. The perspective is slightly wrong, but the main features of the building are clear to see. (By courtesy of the Earl of Pembroke and Montgomery.)

inside may give arms with the best gentleman and never see the herald.' What was happening was that there was growing up a large body of farmers of yeoman (i.e. common) origin who acted purely as owners and managers of farming enterprises, never getting their hands dirty and living in every way as gentlemen. Wealth and position made them gentle. The more successful farmers simply rose *en masse* into the ranks of the lesser gentry. From bondage to gentility in three generations was perfectly feasible. A wealthy farmer such as we speak of is found taking a pride in sending his son to the local grammar school and perhaps even to a university or an inn of court. Very likely, 'the bringing up and marriage of his eldest son is an ambition which afflicts him so soon as the boy is born, and the hope to see his son superior or placed above him drive him to dote upon the boy in his cradle'. Many a gentleman farmer, too, could not be content till he had the outward marks of gentility to set the seal on his success. As Stephens puts it, 'To purchase arms [if he emulates gentry] sets upon him like an ague: it breaks his sleep, takes away his stomach, and he can never be quiet till the herald hath given him the harrows, the cuckoo or some ridiculous emblem for his armoury'. This shows how little human nature changes; but it also demonstrates how economic and social elevation turned yeomen into gentlemen and gentlemen into esquires. This is one of the things that has marked England out from all other nations. Our gentlemen farmers were unique. The most significant thing about the rise of the gentry was this mass rise into the gentry.

On the next rung up the social ladder were the lesser and cultivating landowners, who earned their incomes partly from the rents of their lands and partly from cultivating their own demesnes. Men of this rank were among some of the greatest innovators, especially in the Norfolk Heathlands, the Midland Plain, and the North-eastern Lowlands. The names of Vaughan, Temple, Spencer, and Walpole spring readily to mind. Usually enjoying the status of esquire or knight, such men lived well and were able to enjoy standards undreamt of in earlier times. The luxuries that can be taken as most typical of such persons were less their fine clothing, rich food, plate and jewellery, than the novelties of books, paintings, clocks, watches, and coaches. Above all, it was in buying coaches that men of this kind displayed their new-found wealth to the world. Weather-beaten old diehards might denounce these new contraptions as effeminating; but it was very handy to be able to take the wife and family away for a few days pretty cheaply, and without anyone getting soaked to the skin.

Spreading Prosperity

How lucky and how rich the improvers would have been if only they could have kept to themselves all the great new surpluses created by their own enterprise, industry and ingenuity. But things like that only happen in fairy-tales. In real life, the improvers could only make a profit at all by parting with the major part of their surplus to their various suppliers. As they needed more livestock, their increased demand drove up the price. As they took on more labour, they bid up wages. As they competed for land, they raised rents. As they marketed more, they brought more trade to the merchants. In these and other ways, the superfluity of the improved farms overflowed into people's pockets in all walks of life all over the kingdom.

Heavier stocking of cattle brought increased business at higher prices to other capital farmers in the Lancashire Plain, the Vales of Hereford, and the North-eastern Lowlands, and directly or indirectly to the family farmers of the North, West, and Peak-Forest Countries, Wales and the High Weald. A greater demand for sheep for fatting in fens and marshes and on the new crops and temporary leys increased the takings of family farmers in the hill countries and of all sheep-masters in the Chalk Country and elsewhere who supplied wethers for the folding flocks of so many sheep-and-corn countries, or in-lamb ewes for the house-lamb producers. So great became the demand for sheep, and still more for cattle, that the older sources of supply were outstripped and the stockbreeders of Scotland and Ireland were steadily drawn into the vortex of trade, so that commercial ties were binding all parts of the British Isles into one nation. Improved farming and new crops also stimulated the trade in seeds. Midland farmers bought turnip seed from the Norfolk Heath-lands and clover and ryegrass seeds from the Northdown Country. Seed-corn growers here and in the Polden Hills, the Vale of Pewsey, and other places likewise benefited.

Heightened specialization immediately entailed the growth of trade and so redounded to the advantage of merchants. In particular, many of the metropolitan markets were greatly extended: in the number of transactions and the volumes traded in; in the multitude of participants, and in their scope and sweep. The metropolitan markets in wheat, barley and malt, which had once been restricted to the old cereal-growing and capital-farm countries of the south-east, now pushed further west and north, drawing in the Chalk and Northwold Countries. The market in butter now stretched out to the Vale of Pickering. These and other similar developments were the commercial counterparts of the great agricultural changes of the period, of the deepening and opening up of the divisions of labour, and the triumph of market-minded capitalist farmers. All this made business for the whole-sale merchants, factors, carriers, drovers, bargees, wagon-builders, innkeepers, and the hundred and one others who drew their incomes in whole or in part, directly and indirectly, from the springs of trade. Then, looking a little further afield, we soon see that the growing specializations in different branches of agriculture were accompanied by the widening division of labour between the whole congeries of agricultural industries, and the extractive, processing, transport and manufacturing industries. High farm wages in the great cereal-growing countries dis-couraged the development of manufacturing there. The Chalk, Oxford Heights, Southdown, Northdown, Chiltern, Northwold, and Cotswold Countries became almost purely agricultural, while others were more and more industrialized. The increasing dependence of the Cheese Country on outside grain was due partly to its participation in the West-of-England cloth industry. The expansion of extractive and textile industries in the Peak-Forest Country led it to import butter from the Vale of Pickering. Grain and cheese brought from the Midland Plain to Nottingham and Derby was largely destined to feed industrial workers. The carters brought grain and went away with coal. Corn and coal were likewise exchanged between the Northwold Country and the North-eastern Lowlands and between the Chalk Country and the mines of Mendip. In these and many other ways the growth of the geographical division of labour led to the rise of the middleman.

The Capitalist Landowners

Agricultural improvements showered blessings, too, on agri-cultural landowners. All farmers had to pay rent for the use of the capital they borrowed in the form of farms. This was called the rent of land, but what farmers actually borrowed of their landlords bore the same relation to land in a general sense as does a locomotive to the iron and other mineral ores out of which

it has been made. Farmers hired farmland that had been artificially rendered fertile and productive, constituted in a special
way, and combined with roads, buildings and other works. It
was this capital that farmers borrowed and paid for the use of and
that owner-occupiers enjoyed the imputed rent of by virtue of
acting as their own landlords. This meant that the rent of land
rose and fell according to the demand for and supply not of its
superficial area, but of its capacity to produce income, just as
the interest paid for money capital will rise or fall according to
the profitability of the businesses to which it is devoted. Innovat-
ing, improving and enterprising farmers were emboldened to
offer more for their leases on account of the high profits they
expected. Nobody minds paying a high rate of interest when the
interest-payment is a fleabite compared to the profits. And the
same goes for the rent of land. This explains why it was said of
the farmer, 'If the frowning years should not sometimes diminish
his crop, he would never care what he offered for the hire of
lands'. Or, as John Taylor, the water-poet, put it,

> For if a gentleman hath land to let
> He'll have it, at what price so e'er 'tis set,
> And bids, and overbids, and will give more
> Than any man could make of it before.

There had, however, to be some safeguards and conditions.
The farmer could feel assured that his property in the lease or
farm would be respected. It only remained to secure the fruits of
his enterprise. This was done by paying a lump sum for a lease
long enough to give the enterprising farmer time to recoup
himself and reap the profit of his innovations and improvements.
Only a madman would have thrown his money away in marling,
floating, or making up-and-down land, only to allow someone
else to have the benefit of it all. The practice was therefore adopted
of taking or renewing leases for terms of twenty-one years, or,
what amounted to much the same, for three lives successively.
Then, at the end of seven years, the farmer could bargain for an
extra seven, or, at each death, for a new lease of life. This was
what he had his six or seven years' rent put by for. By this means

farmers could enjoy the profits they earned by their own enterprise.

When they improved their farms, the farmers were nevertheless making permanent improvements in their landlord's lands, and whoever took a lease of them afterwards could naturally expect to pay more rent than before for what was in fact an increased amount of capital in the form of a more highly productive farm. This resulted in farm rents rising higher and higher, as long as wave after wave of innovation made farmers' profits high. Conversely, of course, when innovations died away, rents declined. But this situation only became both prolonged and general about the early eighteenth century. In the meantime, owners of agricultural land were in the happy position of continually gaining capital, and more real capital meant more rent from it. What with the competition, the innovations, and the spreading of prosperity in all directions, rents almost everywhere rose very steeply after 1560, and, except for a setback in the early 1620s, went on rising until 1659.

How innovations drove up rents can be seen clearly by a few examples. In the Midland Plain, converting common-field permanent tillage and grass to grassland enclosures just about doubled the rent of the land. This grazing rent was then redoubled by ploughing up the grass. The landlord simply took a 'ploughing or double rent'. And in up-and-down husbandry this improvement was continuous. 'Grazing fits for ploughing and corning, and corning fits for grazing; a most gallant opportunity: doubles the grazing rent while under corning, and more under woading; and grazeth again immediately after at a very considerable rent.' When meadows are being floated in the Chalk Country, the lessee covenants 'to improve his rent, at the judgment of two indifferent (impartial) men, as the land shall be improved'. Floating in the Vales of Hereford advanced the rents of some fields no less than eight-fold. In the Wealden Vales, as in the Lancashire Plain and the Cheshire Cheese Country, landlords 'let and set such marled grounds under twenty years at an incredible rate of monies in hand'.

When the farmer 'offers the landlord more than he would crave' and 'will give his landlord more than he would ask', when capital gains flowed effortlessly in, the rent-receiver could earn money in his sleep. But the average landlord was no Oblomov and took an active interest in his estates, seeing to it that improvements in husbandry were matched by those in rent. Many landowners, too, joined or assisted in agricultural improvements, participated in floating or enclosure agreements, invested in drainage schemes, or otherwise increased their capital by their own efforts. Then we must bear in mind that very few landowners were owners merely of agricultural land. They often possessed woodlands, coal-mines, iron-works, glass-works, corn, blade, fulling or other mills, fishing rights, inns, industrial dwellings, labourers' cottages, workshops, smithies and all manner of property both rural and urban. The rapid expansion of London, Manchester, Birmingham, Newcastle and other industrial and commercial towns made rents in and near them soar as never before. As such great names as Russell and Grosvenor remind us, town and country planning was the proper function of the private land-owner, and urban landlords, then as now, laid out new residential streets and squares and set up warehouses and shopping arcades. Lastly, the great and middling landowners were not only rural and urban, agricultural and industrial landlords; they often had many other irons in the fire and earned money from their investments in shipping, in trading and mining companies, and from financial transactions and lucrative public officers, so that there were not very many landowners pure and simple. There is not much sense in discussing the standard of living of a supposed class of landowners when their names are listed among the share-holders in the Mines Royal, the East India Company, and the Bank of England. Moreover, even among those men who lived mainly on their rents, there was a wide range right from the highest in the kingdom to the humblest country bumpkin who lived in modest contentment on his single poor manor, or rubbed along on the rents of a few manorial freeholds.

Nevertheless, there were many wealthy landowners, in the sense of men whose incomes came largely from their ownership of landed estates of one kind and another, and when we meet these we almost invariably find that they would have been considerably enriched in this period even if they had no income beyond the rents from their farmers. As for the greatest of these families, it is well known how they luxuriated in fine clothes, sumptuous banquets, stately houses, gold and silver plate, costly jewellery, not to speak of more homely comforts like servants and coaches, and of the patronage of the fine arts and natural sciences. They lived like kings, and much better than most kings.

These great capitalists and landowners drew their incomes from almost every kind and branch of business. This meant that, as a group, they had a sincere and impartial interest in the improvement, growth and development of all industries, trades and occupations. They came thus to represent the general interest rather than particular interests, and the more enlightened and capable of them served as the natural protectors both of their own tenants and of the nation at large. Thus we see John Hervey, the first earl of Bristol, trying to save his tenants at Sleaford from having soldiers billeted on them and to spare Bury St Edmunds from having two troops of dragoons quartered upon it.

The rise of capitalist landownership was clearly an organic part of the development of a nation on the basis of the advanced division of labour. Individual landowning families came and went, and some went from clogs to clogs in three generations. But the great old families mostly stood as strong as oaks, and new ones were recruited from among those who had made money in farming, industry, finance, commerce, politics, and other trades and professions. The more capital was heaped up, the more opportunity there was for persons to acquire it. But what was far more significant, indicative as it was of the essential role of landownership in the life of the nation, was the growing division of labour between farming and landowning, which, incidentally, made room for more landowners, and gave scope for greater ones. Many owner-occupiers sold out to neighbouring landowners with the sole purpose of getting their hands on the working capital needed to exploit opportunities for investment in agriculture on large leasehold farms, the long and easy tenancy of

K

which was often part of the price paid by the new owner of the land. This way the former owner-occupier could now go all out for profit. Such lease-back was the foundation of the business of many a gentleman farmer. When great landowners bought out the small, and when copyholders of inheritance surrendered their customary holdings in return for leases, this was usually to their mutual advantage. This division of labour or separation of functions gave new opportunities to both farmer and landowner, and both their interests were advanced.

The Royal Estates

Capitalist landowners tried to get the best return they could on their capital and to increase the size of their capital holding in the form of landed estates and other real assets. But not all landowners, not even all great landowners, were capitalist ones. The royal estates, in particular, were run in quite a different way. They were divided up and distributed as superior and honourable service-tenancies to royal supporters in return for political and public services, either as a reward for services already rendered to the Crown or as an inducement for such services to be given in the future, or both. To have taken full and improved rents from the captains, courtiers and servants to whom grants of royal land were made, would clearly have defeated the object of the exercise. The rents paid by copyholders and other subtenants were often raised, but this was done only in order to make the superior service-tenancies of which they formed part all the more valuable to their grantees. The implications of this system may perhaps be best grasped if the reader will stretch his imagination so far as to visualize a whole estate of council (or state-owned) houses, all let at purely nominal rents, where the tenancies are in the gift of one man or of a small group of men. Just think what power that man or group would be able to wield in the neighbourhood. Then realize that the Tudor and early Stuart monarchs ran a vast nationwide estate on these very principles and it will soon be understood how they were able to command support.

All this time, as we have seen, rental values were being raised over and over again by competition, improvement and innova-

tion; but the increased rents that on a capitalist estate went to
the landowner, accrued on the royal estates to the superior
service-tenants. One effect of the agricultural revolution, then, in
its earlier and main stages, was to strengthen the power of the
monarchy. Elizabeth, James and Charles I found themselves
with service-tenancies much more valuable than before, more
keenly sought after by suitors, and capable of providing far more
services. The only fly in the ointment was that the inventions
and innovations themselves also gave rise to structural imbalances
in the markets that caused many prices to rise quite steeply for a
long time. Then the Crown, having gained an accession of power
by foregoing higher rents, found itself embarrassed for money to
such an extent that it had to sell off many of its lands and so
forego some of its power in order to make ends meet. In times
of need, however, kings and queens could rely on some help from
church and college estates. These ecclesiastical lands were run in
much the same way as royal estates, with service-tenancies in the
form of 'beneficial leases' being granted to favourites, friends and
relatives as well as to the patrons who had the gift of the various
higher church and academic offices or who were able to help
ambitious place-seekers. This system had what was by some
considered the merit of working well, but it also meant that the
king or queen as supreme head or patron could require grants of
church and college lands for their own use, chiefly for the
creation of service-tenancies depending on themselves. In this
way church and college estates came to form a reserve tank of
service-tenancies that the Crown could switch on when required.
Incidentally, it also meant that the hungry flocks of humble
believers and seekers looked up and were not fed: asking for bread,
they were given a stone.

Working for Wages

The great agricultural changes increased the demand for wage-
labour. Extra hands were needed to form and run the up-and-
down farms, to dig marl and cart it to the fields, to drain the
marshes, to float the meadows, to hoe the turnips, to mow the
hay, and simply to replace petty tenant farmers and share-

croppers. In cereal growing the small farm could not compete on equal terms with the large one. The small farmer had higher unit costs and so little money coming in that he could not wait and get the best prices for what he had to sell. As long as a sellers' market kept corn prices high, all this did not matter so much, but later on, in the seventeenth century, especially towards the end of it, when a buyers' market developed and prices slumped, many small men had to throw up their farms. The situation is rather similar today especially in France and West Germany. With farm produce prices now kept artificially high, however, government agencies intervene to try to get off the land the small man who cannot hope to do much good for himself or anyone else.

This means it is no use asking whether people were better off as wage-workers than they had been as small farmers. As long as they could make a go of their farms, they held on to them. When they could no longer make a go of them, they had to choose other livelihoods. The alternative was thus not between a prosperous little farm and wage-work, but between starvation or pauperism and wage-work. The opportunity to go out to work for wages thus came as a godsend to those who could not make their livings as farmers.

In practice, of course, the contrast between the two callings in life was nowhere near as stark as that. There had long been a wide range of little farms, all the way from the one that gave an ample living to all the family down to the one that was only a part-time living to some of them. Many a small farmer's son went out to work for wages until such time as he could get his own holding, and the others, while waiting for dead men's shoes, were little better than their fathers' hired hands. Besides, many if not most of the farm labourers did a bit of farming for themselves on the side. Casual workers were drawn from the ranks of the cottagers who had their own smallholdings or dwarf farms, half-a-dozen acres or so that they spent some of their time on. Day-labourers and out-dwelling servants usually had some land and kept one or two cows, and a few sheep, pigs, poultry, bees, and so on. Many of them had an acre or two of corn. Shepherds mostly had their own small flocks that they kept with their masters'. Part-time farmers often worked as labourers a good deal of the year. The only utterly landless labourers were the in-dwelling farm servants, and they were saving up to get married and set up house for themselves in a cottage with a few acres and perhaps some common of pasture by right or sufferance. How many young men started their farming careers with one broody hen and a clutch of eggs, we shall probably never know, but it was not infrequent to start with a single ewe or calf and work one's way up. Everyone has to start somewhere, and there was no class or caste of landless wage-labourers in any real or operative sense.

In the event, too, the jump from being in the farming business on one's own account and working in it for someone else was not very great, and most people landed on their feet. When a man found he could no longer make his farm pay, he was still left with several choices. He could be pig-headed, of course, and try to hold on to his team while he found another farm on which to fail again. When a Midland township is enclosed, for example, the family farmers refuse to renew their tenancies because they are unable to meet the rent, and in the nearby town,

'the market is full of enquiry and complaint of such tenants to all they meet, "Can you help me to a farm or a little land to employ my team? I am discharged and if I sell my horses and cattle, I shall never get a team again or so many milk-cows to maintain my family. Also, all my money will be spent that I shall sell them for, ere I shall hear of any land to be set".'

Other men, with better foresight and more agile minds, finding they could no longer make a go of it, and seeing how the growth of trade was creating good openings for carters and carriers, switched their teams from the one industry to the other. Else-where, young men with a bit of gumption, seeing how their fathers moiled and toiled from morn till night for small reward, concluded there must be a better way of making a living and set about finding one. With any luck, something could be salvaged from the farm capital to invest in a workshop, a road wagon, a fishing boat, a set of tools, or anything to get a living by. Some

fathers, wanting their sons to have an easier life than they had
had, would find the money to get them taught a skilled trade or
to set them up in a little business of some kind, knowing full
well, 'It is much easier with the handicrafts labourer that hath a
good trade'. In short, change came not as an all-destroying earth-
quake, but as a series of slight tremors. The writing was on the
wall long enough to give men a chance to heed it, and when one
door shuts, another usually opens.

Besides, when you come to think of it, it was not all beer and
skittles being a struggling and unsuccessful farmer. He worked
on his own account, but was never really his own master: he
could not set his own course but had to go the way the winds
chanced to blow. He toiled all his day, up early and down late,
in all weathers, wearing out himself and his family, in constant
weariness, care and trouble, and beset by worries. A farm
labourer was better off. He had a steady wage and none of the
responsibility. His hours were no longer, possibly shorter, and he
did not have to be a jack-of-all-trades, but could learn the
knack of one or two things until he could do them standing on
his head. At the end of the day he could cast off all cares and
enjoy a few hours of ease, sitting about eating and talking until
bedtime, until eleven o'clock according to a foreign observer. An
unsuccessful farmer who became a wage labourer had lost nothing
but his chains. He could feel for the first time that sense of self-
reliance, sturdy independence, security, and serenity that comes
from regular employment at a steady wage. The idea that free
wage labour was somehow degrading would probably never have
occurred to an impoverished tenant farmer.

It has to be appreciated that in those days there was no such
things as mass unemployment, least of all in the countryside.
Farmers never tired of complaining how difficult it was to find
workers. All the indications are that the demand for labour
exceeded the supply and that vacancies could soon have been
found for all those who offered their services, since it seems to
have been chiefly the shortage of wage-workers that prevented
more capital farms being set up. This was largely because there
were so many part-time industrial jobs that families could take

and combine with part-time farming. At certain times, labour shortages and wage-costs became a perfect nightmare to the farmers, and we can readily sense that careless attitude to work shown by men who know there will always be another job for them to go to. This was especially marked in times of boom, like the first two decades of the seventeenth century, when the demand for labour greatly exceeded the supply. James Bankes of Winstanley complains, 'I have been hindered by keeping of servants in getting of corn, so that I have rather desired to die than to live, for they care not whether end go forward, so that they have meat, drink and wages. Small fear of God is in servants.' Robert Loder of Harwell found the same. 'All workmen almost', he complains, 'will play legerdemain with their masters and favour themselves . . .; men can work when they list and so they can loiter.' It was the same story everywhere: full employment gave men the whip hand over their masters. About 1655 things went from bad to worse. Farm servants, it was said 'are grown so proud and idle that the master cannot be known from the servant. They are like ere long to be masters, and their masters servants, many poor husbandmen being forced to pay near as much to their servants for wages as to their landlords for rent'. Then at the end of the century, we are told, 'plough servants first began to exalt their dominion over their masters'.

That poor, struggling, insolvent corn-growers found going out to work for wages repugnant or that their lot in life was worsened by so doing, is unbelievable. Some may have had a prejudice against working for someone else, but that is not quite the same thing. Some may even have said they did not like going out to work, but this makes no odds. Saying is not paying. People's wishes are shown best by what they choose to do, and the fact is that more and more chose to go out and work for wages rather than struggle along as their own masters.

Farm Workers' Wages. All farm workers were paid some of their wages in money, but hardly any of them wholly in money. Many farm servants lived-in with their masters, with board and lodging and all found. The wages of such in-dwelling servants were thus more akin to a soldier's pay than to wages as generally understood nowadays. Wages were not what a man had to keep himself on, but what he had left over when all his keep had been provided for. The upshot was, a single man living in with his master could save most of his wages towards setting up house or even making the down payment on a small holding of land, while the milkmaid, whose face is her fortune (cowpox having immunised her against smallpox), 'bestows her year's wages at next fair . . . in choosing her garments'.

Not only in-dwelling servants, but all farm workers took their wages partly in kind, even if only by way of bonuses and fringe benefits. A shepherd would have free pasture for a score or so of sheep, a free coat, ten bushels each of rye and oats, keep for a cow and a calf, a tied cottage at a nominal rent, and a supply of firewood, perhaps free ploughing and folding on a few common-field acres, and all tails docked from the sheep. And over and above all this, a shepherd had plenty of un-occupied time and did not spend it all playing his pipe. He might also make straw hats or something else for sale. An out-dwelling carter or ploughman would have his money wages, but also a tied cottage, a kitchen garden, a supply of faggots, four bushels of wheat, four weeks full board during harvesting, keep for a hog, and all the horsehair trimmed off. Another husbandman would have allowances of seed barley and oats and land to sow them on, the loan of a horse to ride to market, beanstraw for kindling, free fruit and vegetables, and keep for a few sheep and cattle. Constant day-labourers would be allowed a cottage and garden and keep for a pig. Some servants were given full liveries of grey frieze and a pair of boots. Others took cash in lieu and bought their own clothing, but nevertheless received bonuses that included a hempen shirt, a pair of shoes, a supply of knitting wool, an apron or smock, and an old suit, hat or pair of breeches. Money wages were the basic or minimum; bonuses and fringe benefits were what people kept their eye on. The 'good em-ployer' who had the pick of the labour market, was the man whose servants could 'uncontrolled find the highway to the cupboard' and who won 'the name of a bountiful yeoman' by his bonuses in kind. The fringe benefit most generally enjoyed by farm-workers, however, and the one they set most store on, was that of being allowed to buy all the farm produce they needed for themselves at special concessionary rates from their employers, at least at the lowest seasonal farmgate price, and very often well below that.

The governments of the day operated, with varying degrees of efficiency, an incomes policy so transparently farcical that the regulated assessments reflected what were the going rates. Both from these assessments and from records of payments actually made, we can get a rough idea of the kind of rates that were paid at various times, and see that they generally shifted upwards in unison with other prices. But the rates at which wages were paid are not much guide to money earnings. The rates applicable to servants were graduated according to the different grades of farm labour. One way of increasing a man's earnings was thus to upgrade him from the 'worst sort' of servant to the 'middling sort' or the 'best sort'. As for day-labourers, what mattered was clearly less the daily rate than the number of days worked. To calculate earnings and changes in earnings is, therefore, difficult if not impossible. Even then, the figures would be for money earnings only, and these are meaningless until translated into purchasing power. What the various money earnings would purchase in terms of goods in different places at different times is what we need to know, but almost impossible to find out. Even if we could find out, it might not help much, because different people want to buy different things at different times in different quantities on different terms in different places. In view of the fact that earnings were taken only partly in money, however, none of these difficulties matters much.

The best we can do, then, is to try to form a rough and ready notion of what people's real earnings were from their styles and standards of living, in rather the same way as we did previously for the landowners and well-to-do farmers.

How Poor Folks Lived
A day-labourer or out-dwelling servant often had rather a

spartan life, but very much depended on individual circumstances that defy generalization. Plain, coarse and often threadbare clothing and sparse household furniture, consisting largely of stools, trestle tables and flockbeds, were the general rule. But in sober truth there is not, and never was, any such thing as a single, general standard of living among wage-workers. An airline pilot does not live like a railway porter, nor did a chief servant in husbandry live like an unskilled labourer. Different styles of life can be seen perhaps most clearly from a few of the many kinds of labourers' and servants' cottages. The luckier or abler people who had managed to save up some money could hope to get an old-established cottage-holding with its own rights of common and a few acres of land. To take one example out of thousands, in 1629 Ellis Ellyot had managed to put down £8 to get the lease for three lives of a cottage at Burcombe, in the Chalk Country. In return for his two shillings a year he now had a dwelling house of three ground rooms, two of which were lofted over. This made, say, three living rooms, including the kitchen, and two bedrooms, which was plenty for himself, his wife and two sons, and would do for a larger family. Outside there was a useful barn, a 'backside' or courtyard, six perches of garden ground, plenty big enough for herbs and vegetables, and four acres of land in the common fields, two in one and one in each of the two others. He could have this cultivated by a jobbing ploughman, if the farmer he worked for would not do it as a bonus or favour, and so grow enough corn for bread and ale, with some left over for the chickens, and some straw for the cow. With his own cow, a few pigs, poultry, and a hive of bees, and his wife doing some spinning for the clothier, the family could live fairly comfortably. As the family grew, housekeeping would cost more, but by then the elder boys could start earning a little money by weeding, bird-scaring or some such.

At the bottom of the scale, another farm worker might have to content himself with a cottage on the waste, perhaps one he had built himself with the special permission of the lord of the manor. This would very likely have been thrown up in a day or two. It would consist of a single bay between two pairs of main timbers and so contain only one room, which, at first at least, would not be lofted over. The roof would be thatched with straw and the walls made of mud or clay, strengthened with straw perhaps, and faced with plaster. A man could say he had his family between four walls with a roof over their heads, but not much more. Outside there would be nothing beyond a little kitchen garden and a necessary house at the bottom of it. One would have to rely on the charity of the commoners in closing their eyes to an extra cow going on their pastures. Not all commoners were so kind-hearted, and some were not above pulling down cottages built on the waste if they thought them a nuisance. It only took a rope and a cart-horse or two to topple such a cabin, and it was all done in a flash. Even if all went well, it was not much of a prospect to try to bring up a family in a single room measuring at the most about 250 square feet and very likely as little as 120 or even 80. But these were the poorest of the poor labourers or impoverished widow women who lived in such hovels.

Even the poor day-labourer in his cabin on the waste was better off than some folk. Shortage of housing in some parts meant that some unfortunates were 'like to lie in the street', and elsewhere church-houses had to be taken over as emergency quarters or reception centres. Or consider what befell one Barton of Winstanley, near Wigan. Another tenant took his house over his head and put him out, together with his wife and children, so that 'he was constrained to make a poor cabin without the house and enforced to life upon the ground a whole winter', watched all the time by his pitiless evictor and relying for necessities on collections taken up by his neighbours. It was something to be thankful for to have a proper roof over your head.

Servants who lived-in faced no such housing problems. They were usually quartered over the stables, cowhouse or some similar outbuilding. They could thus enjoy the benefits of a primitive kind of underfloor heating, as in a Swiss chalet. Dairymaids sometimes had feather beds, but otherwise the furniture consisted of flock beds on trestled bedboards, with blankets and coverlets, and perhaps a cupboard and a stool.

Living conditions were thus similar to those enjoyed by the most comfortably placed solders in the last war. Sometimes the lofts over the outhousing gave insufficient room for the servants, and then employers often built special low chambers or houses for them. This was common practice in the Chalk Country. In 1632 the farmer of Stoke Farthing demesne had an out-chamber for servants to lodge in and his opposite number at Bishopstone had one ground room as a similar lodging chamber. In 1597 the Amesbury demesne farmer asks his landlord that 'a convenient house may be erected for harbouring such labouring men as must be always employed'.

All husbandmen wore clothing that seemed very plain and dull to the city dandy or the courtier or the great landowner. In Edmund Spenser's *Mother Hubbard's Tale* the travellers were nothing surprised when

> At last they chanc'd to meet upon the way
> A simple husbandman in garments grey;
> Yet though his vesture were but mean and base,
> A good yeomen he was of honest place,
> And more for thrift did care than for gay clothing.

Even quite well-to-do farmers ordinarily wore plain, sensible clothes. So, for that matter, did the wealthy Dutch burghers of this period. When we read about the husbandman's garments being dull and colourless, we have to imagine the terms in which popular entertainers and coffee-bar cowboys would describe a bank manager's business suit. All it means is that farmers were not dandies.

As for farm workers, most of them would usually have worn clothing that was not only plain and severe, but also often shabby and dirty. In this they would have been no different from most other working people. As they had a dirty job to do, they were content to wear a good deal of old and cast-off clothing, just as similar people do nowadays. But this does not mean they were not well and warmly clad. A typical farm worker's wardrobe might be made up something like this: brogue shoes, made of undressed leather with the original hair turned inside; 'start-ups' (ankle-boots), high shoes, or half-boots, all of which were usually slit and laced after the fashion of modern lace-ups; stout, tab-fastened top-boots; woollen stockings; loose, baggy breeches, a cloak, and a hooded cape, all made of 'homespun' or 'russet', or of frieze, Kendal green or some other cheap, serviceable woollen cloth, or perhaps of linsey-woolsey, which was a mixture of linen and wool, or of some other fustian or part-wool fabric; a quilted woollen doublet; a sleeveless sheepskin or leather jerkin; a moleskin waistcoat; a canvas smock, linen shirts, and lockram (light linen) underwear. The outer clothing would largely have been made to measure by a local tailor, though unfortunately not always for the man who was wearing it now. Jerkins, and some other items, were bought in stock sizes. The shirts and underwear might well be home-made (*plates 24, 25, 26, 27, 28, 29, 30*). The footwear could have been made to measure or, more likely, bought in stock sizes. It was made of thick, heavy leather, similar to that used by farmers and soldiers nowadays, the employment of calf-skin being regarded as a fraudulent practice. All shoes and boots were, of course, soled in leather, and many or most of them were double soled like modern veld-schoen. It was the only way field shoes could be made waterproof. If the mire was very bad, pattens (galoshes) were sometimes worn in addition to shoes or boots. These pattens were wooden soles or undershoes with rings around their rims so that they could be tied over the shoe or boot. Wooden shoes or clogs may have been worn in some places or on some occasions, but were not in general use. They were associated in the popular mind with backward continental countries. Hence the cry, 'No popery, no wooden shoes'. This slogan may have been unfair, but certainly what most obviously distinguished the English farm labourer from the European peasant was that the one was well shod and the other was not. It soon began to shock English travellers in Scotland and abroad to see people going about barefoot.

Clothing differed much from place to place in those days, because local tailors and shoemakers had their own particular ways of doing things. It varied also between job and job, even among farm workers. Take, for instance, the Chalk Country shepherd. He wore a long white cloak with an extra deep cape made of locks of wool straight from the sheep's back. We have to picture him off to the bleak downs in the depth of winter with his dog, his sheep-crook, sling, tar-box, scrip or pouch, and his pipe or flute, to spend days and nights with his flock in a little cabin by the sheepcote. He stood in more need of warm clothing than anybody.

The staff of life was bread, but the farmworkers had as their other staples of diet: beef, mutton, cheese and vegetables. They did not always have wheaten bread, but the rye-bread, oatcakes, barley bannocks and loaves of maslin (mixed wheat and rye), which were the alternatives, were nearly as good. Rye has almost as much protein as wheat, and oats and barley only a quarter and a third less. All have about the same proportion of starch, except for oats, which make up for it with more fat. But farm labourers and servants did not generally consume oats, for the hill countries where they were most eaten were precisely the ones where there were hardly any farm workers. In-dwelling servants fared hardly worse than their masters. Those who were with working farmers might sit at a separate table, but it was in the same room and had much the same food on it. In the Northwold Country, for example, the Best family ate bread made of barley, rye and peas, and wheatmeal pastry. Their servants had the same bread, but maslin piecrusts and barleymeal puddings, except at harvest time, or when there was plenty of tail or poor-quality wheat, when wheatmeal was substituted. Wherever wheat was a main crop it was used for the bread of masters and servants alike and eaten by both in ample quantities. In Robert Loder's household each man consumed about a peck of wheat wholemeal in bread every week, and about seven tenths of a peck of barley malted and brewed into beer. Each had, too, a good deal of butchers' meat and bacon, about a quarter of a pound of cheese, some butter, milk, fish and fruit. Every day a man could expect two pounds of genuine wholemeal bread, with all the germ of the grain in it, some high-protein food, including meat, and some vegetables, all washed down with half a gallon

of beer. Both men and maid-servants everywhere habitually
expected roast meat for supper twice a week, and this supper was
taken at seven or eight o'clock in the evening, and was a lighter
meal than their dinner, which they took at noon. Fresh or
preserved peas, beans, carrots, cabbages, and turnips were also
much eaten in all places.

Naturally, the exact fare provided varied considerably from
place to place and from season to season. In Lent, fish largely
replaced flesh. Butchers' and pork butchers' meat was often
supplemented or replaced by rabbits, hares, larks, bustards and
other common game. Early modern Englishmen felt no more
compunction than modern Italians in taking larks, peewits, and
other singing birds in nets to cook in pies. Indeed, the nursery
rhyme about blackbirds baked into a pie is no way far fetched.
Eggs and milk were readily available most of the year, but were
presumably consumed rather less in winter. Then there were all
the cultivated, orchard and soft fruits, and nuts, and wild straw-
berries, blackberries, sloes, elderberries, beech-nuts, chestnuts,
and much else to be picked and collected by the countryman and
woman.

The in-dwelling servants usually did quite well in the matter of
food and drink. Indeed, they were almost certainly better off in
this respect than the vast majority of poor tenant farmers in the
self-same districts, for the latter were said to be glad of a bit of
hanged bacon once a week and were rarely able to afford fresh
meat. Farmers were willing to feed their servants well in order to
get good and willing labour, but small tenant farmers could only
fare well themselves by foregoing sales in the market that they
could ill do without. And, what amounts to much the same thing,
these same servants are generally regarded as having fed better
than the average fifteenth-century husbandman on his own little
farm. Looking at their diets in another way, they appear to have
been considerably better than those of most unemployed men
and their wives in the 1930s, and slightly superior to those of
persons of middling income in the years before the last war.

We know far less about the diets of out-dwelling servants and
day-labourers, but have every reason to suppose that they fed

as well as farm servants who were living in. After all, the servants who lived out were mostly those who had lived in when they were single, and we can hardly suppose that married men who survived the first few weeks of their wives' cooking generally fared worse than unmarried ones. As for the day-labourers, it is equally unlikely that they were worse off than the servants, except in that their fortunes fluctuated more; for if day-labourers had been substantially worse off than servants, the supply of the former would probably have dried up as that of the latter increased. Besides, as we have seen, both outdwelling servants and day-labourers obtained free or cut-price foodstuffs from their employers. Furthermore, most of them had their own cows, pigs, poultry and kitchen gardens and some their own small holdings or dwarf farms.

All in all, then, it appears that farm workers lived rather better than their neighbours who were struggling family farmers. This is hardly surprising. Capital farms with wage-workers were more productive than the competing family farms, and their workers were more specialized and expert. Above all, if farm labourers had not been rather better off than struggling family farmers, no one would have preferred wage-work to self-employment, whereas in fact increasing numbers did exactly this.

Agriculture and Industry

To appreciate properly how much standards of living improved for the population as a whole, it is necessary to glance at changes that took place at this time in industries other than agriculture.

First, the increased production of industrial crops which was part and parcel of the agricultural revolution, encouraged some industrial expansion. The cultivation of saffron (*plate 9*) and in growing quantities, of madder, weld, and especially of woad (*plate 8*), which was used both for blues and for the foundation for dark colours, provided more raw material for the dyers. The spread of cole-seed (*plate 7*), cultivation was associated with the rise of the seed-crushing industry, which in turn supplied oil for soap-making, for burning in lamps, and for use in the textile industries. More sheep meant more raw material for parchment-makers, glovers, and cloth-makers. Increased numbers of cattle gave larger supplies of materials to the tanners, shoemakers, saddlers, horners, spectacle-makers and many others.

The most important development of this kind stemmed from the rise of the pasture sheep of the Midland Plain, the Fen Country, the North-eastern Lowlands and elsewhere. These sheep gave far more wool than their predecessors had done, and wool of quite a different kind. The pasture wool was long and straight and silky. It was also coarse and strong as compared with the wool of arable sheep from common and fallow fields. Wool from these fallow sheep was naturally curly and it was carded before it was spun up, that is, the original strands were confused and entangled as much as possible. It then made up into soft-faced woollen cloth. But pasture wool had no curl to start with and, instead of being carded, was combed out as long and straight as possible, thus enhancing its natural qualities and producing a strong, smooth yarn. This was then woven up into a lighter worsted cloth in which the threads were still visible on a hard surface. Most mens' suits are now made in this worsted fashion, which will perhaps be most easily recognized under the name of serge, which is one of its many forms. Spun in a different way, pasture wool is also made up into jersey or knitting wool. The worsted industry had long existed alongside the woollen manufacture, but with the huge increase in the growth of pasture wool from 1560 onwards, the manufacture of serges and other worsteds was enormously increased, and at the same time new materials were invented that included both carded and combed wool and were called new draperies or half-worsteds, because they were new and half made of worsted yarns. There thus grew up a much extended range of light-weight materials that could be used for a number of purposes for which the old woollen cloths were much too heavy.

Secondly, the growing profitability of agriculture, and, later, the rise of population made possible by improved food supplies, encouraged important developments in the coal industry and, indirectly, elsewhere. As we have seen, the agricultural improvers bid up the rents of farm land. They did this to such an extent that

L

landowners found it better to clear their woodlands for agricultural purposes. The demand for fuel was meanwhile greatly increased by the much larger needs of various industries, among which may be mentioned cheese-making and iron-working. Under these circumstances, new opportunitities were created for the mining, sale and use of coal fuel, provided that its production could be raised without pushing its cost up much. This was achieved by a technical revolution in which surface digging was replaced by deep mining, which involved coal-workings on a very much larger scale and great investments of capital. So took place the justly famous rise of the British coal industry. Coal production increased about fourteen-fold between 1551–60 and 1681–90 and the fuel market was completely transformed. Then each industry that took to using coal fuel had to re-equip accordingly, and domestic users had to modernize their homes in order to burn coal. As the greater part of the coal sold was sea-borne, there was also an immense expansion of coastal shipping and inland navigation.

Thirdly, the swelling of farm profits, wages and rents created a vast new volume of demand from a mass of eager consumers. As their incomes rose, people developed new tastes and wants and what had been luxuries now came to be regarded as necessities.

Fourthly, the saving of labour in agriculture, by the introduction of further large-scale working and other means, made a great number of hands free, willing and able to engage in mining, processing, manufacturing and other industries.

Thus the agricultural improvements, directly or indirectly, created, or helped to create, the supply of and the demand for a whole new range of consumers' goods. The changes in agriculture and other industries complemented each other, formed part of one whole organic process, could not have occurred apart, and cannot be understood in isolation from each other.

An Age of Affluence

As they now produced more, English people now consumed more. Production mounted steadily and people in all walks of life were able to enjoy new comforts and little extras in the happy security of the knowledge that there was plenty more where that came from. It had only to be got by industry and inventiveness.

It would be useless to ask which class or classes of persons were the chief beneficiaries of these waves of improvement. To all intents and purposes Tudor and Stuart England was in the last stages of becoming a free and open society without any set caste or class system. The last bastions of privilege were rapidly falling, and the last of all was destroyed by the civil war of the 1640s. When asked who gained from higher and better production, we can only answer, Why, the consumers of course, who else but the whole mass of consumers? Irrespective of whether they were wage-workers or employers, whether they were in this industry or that, whether they were rich or poor, all consumers stood to gain.

Food improved. Consumers now enjoyed, winter and summer, more fresh meat, cheese and butter than ever before. Rich people had had these things a long time; they had been produced in relatively small quantities at comparatively high prices. Now they were made available to far greater numbers at relatively low prices. Even the poorest farm worker now had a diet superior to the one he or his ancestors had put up with before. As poor people began to find they could afford to buy wheat, they gave up eating rye or mixed wheat-and-rye or barley bread. In south-eastern parts of England the turning point came in the 1620s. Then 'the poorer sort that would have been glad but a few years before of the coarse rye-bread, did usually traverse the markets to find out the finer wheats'. Englishmen now 'lost their rye teeth' for ever. Further west, in and about the Cotswold Country, this kind of change came somewhat later. John Aubrey recalled, 'Till the beginning of the civil wars wheat was rarely sown hereabout, and the brown bread was barley. Now [about 1670] all the servants and poor people eat wheaten bread'. The real price of beer also fell, and the small beer or 'pritch', which was beer of the second water, rather like tea from a refilled pot, being only some 8d a barrel, flowed more freely than water itself.

Clothing improved. A greater variety of worsted and half-

L*

worsted materials was being produced at prices increasingly
within the reach of servants and others of the poorer sort. 'The
ploughman', we are told by Thomas Lodge, 'must nowadays
have his doublet of the fashion with wide cuts, his garters of fine
silk of Granada, to meet his Sis on Sundays'. At the time of the
Restoration, we are told that formerly 'gentlewomen esteemed
themselves well clothed in a serge gown which a chambermaid
would now be ashamed to be seen in'. By the beginning of the
next century, material had been so cheapened that 'ladies of the
best quality began to appear in a gown and petticoat under
twenty-five shillings, till the meanness of the price giving every
servant an opportunity to be as fine as her mistress, it grew a
little obsolete among the women; then the men fell into it.'
(Defoe) The milkmaid now followed a much more fickle fashion
on her trips to the fairs. Men paid less attention to such matters,
but their clothing improved, even if in spite of themselves. The
complaint became 'that the master cannot be known from the
servant, except it be because the servant wears better clothes than
the master', and this was spoken of farmers and farm-servants.
Knitting wool, too, now became cheaper, and women took to
knitting things for themselves and their families or, sometimes,
for the market. Shepherdesses knitted for sale as they watched
the flocks. Then, at the turn of the sixteenth and seventeenth
centuries, machine-knitting started. One way and another,
knitwear became cheap and plentiful, forcing some erstwhile
market hand-knitters to switch to lace making. Knitwear partly
displaced woven goods, especially for purposes for which it was
clearly better. Thus cut cloth hose gave way to knitted stockings
even among the poorest people. And then in the seventeenth
century cheap Indian cotton goods started to flood in and clothing prices fell faster and further than ever.

Housing improved. In the previous age the ordinary man 'made
his fire against a reredos (brick or stone back) in the hall, where
he dined and dressed his meat', while the smoke rose to the roof
and found its way out through loopholes. Hence the 'smoky
rafters' of the shepherd's cottage in Milton's Comus. Now people
built themselves chimneys to take away the smoke. In south-east

England chimneys were sprouting up in the 1560s and 1570s as fast as television aerials in the 1950s (*Plates 12, 31, 32, figure 16*). Harrison in 1587 noted 'the multitude of chimneys lately erected' and recalls the time when chimneys were seen only on manor houses and the best mansion houses. Further north people tended to be a step behind the southerners. As late as 1576 most houses in the Cheshire Cheese Country still had their fires in the middle, and it was only between then and about 1616 that their owners built on chimneys. By the end of the seventeenth century one had to go to Scotland, or almost as far, to find houses without chimneys and with smoke billowing about inside everywhere. These new-fangled chimneys would have been a great luxury for humble people in the ordinary course of events, but now the use of coal fires made them a necessity. Wood smoke could be tolerated, coal smoke could not. Having thus funnelled the smoke out through the roof, people could now fit out their houses accordingly. Since the roof was no longer full of smoke, it could be lofted over and converted into bedrooms. These needed dormer windows cut through the roof, and the most economic way of going about this was to have both chimney and windows fitted at the same time (*plates 31, 32 figure 16*). Having done all this, it was a shame not to go the whole hog and have all the windows glazed. In former times glass windows had been a rarity only to be found in churches and in the best rooms of gentlemen's houses. Elsewhere people made do with a leather curtain, a wooden shutter, or perhaps a sheet of thin horn. Now new glass-works were started up for making cheap window-glass. The first one was set up in the south-east in the 1560s and others followed step by step as the glass-makers moved west and north exploiting the market further and further afield, district by district, keeping transport and sales within manageable areas. In the south-east, Harrison in 1587 already noted the rapid spread of window-panes. In the Cheese and Cotswold countries they were still hardly known in the early seventeenth century and poor people were still without them in 1640, but by 1671 they were everywhere to be seen in all classes of houses. At this time windows in the Vales of Hereford and thereabouts were still mostly unglazed, but several glass-works that would soon remedy this were already going up. And so this steady progress moved northward until window-glass became common all over England. It made houses incomparably more comfortable and everyone benefited by it, even the poorest. 'Now the poorest people that are upon alms have it', says Aubrey in 1671. It was in much this way, too, that chimneys had been spread, following in the wake of the new and often coal-fired brickworks. Housing in the hilly and stony countries had long been made of stones and slate of course, and continued to be so. In the lowlands and clay vales, bricks and tiles now came into their own as the materials for new or rebuilt houses. Many minor improvements, too, became possible, with bricks and tiles. If the earthen floors had not been boarded over, they could now be bricked in. Thatch was torn down to be used as compost and replaced by tiles (*plates 13, 31, figure 16*). In these and other ways people set about modernizing their old houses and building new and better ones.

People's lives were improved in many and various ways. Servants and labourers now threw out their straw paillasses and took over the flock beds discarded by their betters in favour of feather ones. Currants and raisins were imported and sold more widely in the seventeenth century. Tobacco, at first mainly grown in the Vale of Evesham, later Virginian, was marketed at prices within reach of ordinary pockets (*plate 10*), and cheap clay pipes were made to smoke it in. The humblest farmworker could now enjoy a quiet smoke with his jar of beer at the end of the day, and there is a good deal of evidence that some of them smoked as they went about their work; otherwise it would hardly have been necessary to forbid smoking near haystacks and cornricks. This, too, was perhaps the age of the rise of games and sports. We hear more now of cricket, stoolball, football, skittles and cudgels. Little is known as yet of these neglected but highly significant aspects of English history. We do not know, for example, how far poor men and boys played cricket, though they certainly did stoolball. John Smyth tells us, 'Gentry, yeomanry, rascality, boys and children do take part in a game called "stoball" '. And this was a merry, lively England even for poor country people. Morris and other dancing was popular—''Tis merry in hall when beards wag all.' We read of farm men and maid-servants making merry at the local victualler's, feasting on roast veal, 'whitepot' and other delicacies to the accompaniment of minstrelsy. It was, too, as far as can be seen, an increasingly healthy England. More fresh foods and more meat meant greater stamina and more resistance to infections. 'The brick-built house with its slated or tiled roof . . . was probably the most important single factor in the eventual disappearance of the house rat from the bulk of England.' (Shrewsbury.) And the disappearance of the house rat meant the disappearance of the plague. It went out with the revolution in agriculture, the early industrial revolution, and the growing affluence. Plague could not survive in an England well fed and well housed.

All the betterment of life we have spoken of may seem very slight by the standards of today, but it was relatively great for those times. Brick chimneys, glass windows, coal fires, dormer bedrooms were the equivalent then of central heating and double glazing today; the new fresh foods of quick-frozen vegetables; half-worsteds and knitwear of man-made fibres; and tobacco of television.

The industry and enterprise of the age of the agricultural revolution resulted in the one thing that could fully justify it, in the one thing that only free private enterprise can provide—the betterment of the neediest members of the community, the true welfare of the common people, the only real and lasting relief of the lot of the poor.

Suggestions for Further Reading

L. A. Clarkson, *The Pre-Industrial Economy in England, 1500–1750.*

Eric Kerridge, *The Agricultural Revolution.*

Eric Kerridge, *Agrarian Problems in the Sixteenth Century and After.*

J. U. Nef, *The Conquest of the Material World.*

C. Wilson, *England's Apprenticeship.*

Index